Personality Development through the Life Span

Life-Span Human Development Series

Series Editors: Freda Rebelsky, Boston University, and Lynn Dorman

Personality Development through the Life Span

Barbara M. Newman

The Ohio State University

Philip R. Newman

with the assistance of
Luan Wagner Stewart

The Ohio State University

BROOKS/COLE PUBLISHING COMPANY
MONTEREY, CALIFORNIA

Printed in the United States of America

10   9   8   7   6   5   4   3   2   1

Library of Congress Cataloging in Publication Data

Newman, Barbara M
    Personality development through the life span.

    (The Brooks/Cole life-span human development series)
    Bibliography: p.
    Includes index.
    1. Developmental psychology.   2.   Personality.
I.   Newman, Philip R., joint author.   II.   Stewart,
Luan Wagner, joint author.   III.   Title.
BF713.N49   155.2'5   80-14291
ISBN 0-8185-0380-7

Acquisition Editor: *Todd Lueders*
Manuscript Editor: *Rephah Berg*
Production Editor: *Sally Schuman*
Series Design: *Linda Marcetti*
Cover Photo: *Karen R. Preuss*
Cover Design: *Ruth Scott*
Illustrations: *John Foster*
Typesetting: *TriStar Graphics, Minneapolis, Minnesota*

Series Foreword

What are the changes we see over the life span? How can we explain them? And how do we account for individual differences? The Life-Span Human Development Series provides a new way to look at these questions. It approaches human development from three major perspectives: (1) a focus on basic issues related to the study of life-span developmental psychology, such as methodology and research design, cross-cultural and longitudinal studies, age-stage phenomena, and stability and change; (2) a focus on age divisions—infancy, early childhood, middle childhood, adolescence, young and middle adulthood, and late adulthood; and (3) a focus on developmental areas such as physiology, cognition, language, perception, sex roles, and personality.

There is some overlap in the content of these volumes. We believe that it will be stimulating to the reader to think the same idea through from the viewpoints of different authors or from the viewpoints of different areas of development. For example, language development is the subject of one volume and is also discussed in the volume on cross-cultural development, among others.

Instructors and students may use the entire series for a thorough survey of life-span developmental psychology or, since each volume can be used independently, may choose selected volumes to cover specific concept areas or age ranges. Volumes that focus on basic issues can be used to introduce the student to the life-span concept.

No single author could adequately cover the entire field as we have defined it. Our authors found it exciting to focus on their areas of specialization within a limited space while, at the same time, expanding their thinking to encompass the entire life span. It can be beneficial to both author and student to attempt a new integration of familiar material.

Since we think it also benefits students to see ideas in development, we encouraged the authors not only to review the relevant literature but also to use what they now know to point up possible new areas of study. As a result, the student will learn to think about human development rather than just learn the facts of development.

Freda Rebelsky

Lynn Dorman

Preface

This book provides a special opportunity to concentrate on the relation between concepts from the field of developmental psychology and concepts from the field of personality. We expect that you will find the challenge of integrating these two broad perspectives very stimulating. It requires careful selection of those themes from the two areas that are most vivid, robust, and compelling. We hope you will enjoy confronting some of the most meaningful and thought-provoking issues of human development.

First we develop a working definition of personality from the theoretical literature; this definition is presented in Chapter 1. Then we proceed to discuss concepts that are of particular interest to developmental psychologists with a life-span perspective and to those interested in the scientific study of personality. These topics—temperament, talent, motivation, social roles, and coping styles—are analyzed in Chapters 2, 3, 4, and 5.

In each of these chapters, special attention is given to the relation between the concepts of personality and life-span developmental psychology. Two implications that emerge from these analyses are discussed. One implication is that the self-concept becomes the conceptual habitat for personality. The second implication is that the self-concept guides the development of one's personality.

To clarify the relation between concepts of personality and life-span developmental psychology, in Chapter 6 we have discussed three studies in which researchers have had an opportunity to study the same subjects over long periods of their lives. One study took place in the East, one in the Midwest, and one in the far West. As a group, these studies begin to provide an understanding of some of the questions raised in a life-span analysis of the study of personality. In particular they provide insight about stability and change, about maturation and socialization, and about growth and regression. Chapter 7 is an analysis of the self-concept, showing the relation between personality and the development of a personal conception of one's self.

Many people have contributed their time and talent in the preparation of this book. The project was supported in part by a faculty development grant from Russell Sage College. Judy Woodall and Susan Kugel provided technical assistance at various stages of preparation. Sara Twitty and Ethel Levin typed the manuscript. We would like to thank our colleagues, David Shaffer of the University of Georgia and Maryann Bishop Coffey of the University of Pittsburgh, who gave us their comments about the manuscript. We are especially grateful to Freda Rebelsky and Lynn Dorman for asking us to contribute to the series and for their encouragement and advice at every step of preparation. We want to thank Todd Lueders and our friends at Brooks/Cole for all their help. Finally, we have thoroughly enjoyed our collaboration with Luan Wagner Stewart.

Barbara M. Newman
Philip R. Newman

Contents

Chapter One

Introduction

Personality Development through the Life Span? What an audacious title for a short book! How can one possibly hope to cover the topic of personality development in one brief volume, to say nothing of trying to offer a life-span perspective of this most elusive of psychological concepts? We hope you will think of this book as the beam of a flashlight that you use to find your way through the woods on a dark night. You know that the beam does not illuminate the whole woods. It simply serves to guide you along the path. As you walk along, you will see some things in sharp detail and others as a shadowy blur. You must keep in mind the selectivity of the beam as you travel. Ideally, the ideas that you encounter here will spark your own journeys, wandering along different paths. Most important, the book will raise a set of difficult questions. In no way is this project seen as a summary, a conclusion to all that has been said about personality. Instead, it is viewed as a stimulus for new thoughts.

A Working Definition of Personality

Consider for a moment the concept of personality. What does it mean to you, how would you define it? Every major psychological theory has offered its own view of the important components of personality and the process of personality formation. In addition to these formal theories, there are a variety of implicit theories that reflect the desire to make predictions about people on the basis of their behavior. In order to pursue the study of personality, we have to begin with an agreed-on definition of the term—a set of limits to it. We offer this working definition as a way of focusing attention on the main areas of concern. After reading the rest of the book, you may decide that the definition is inadequate or that no such thing as personality really exists. Until that point, we invite you to lean on our definition and see whether it will bear the weight of further inquiry.

Personality is that relatively consistent set of thoughts, feelings, and behavior patterns that guide the organization of experience and the direction of new growth. The word *personality* is a general term that represents the integration of four major factors: traits and talents; motives; roles; and coping style. Together these factors contribute to a configuration that is recognizable to the self from within and to others as observers, and it is this that we call "personality." Traits and talents provide unique areas of competence and unique predispositions toward or away from particular events. Motives contribute a set of goals for action, a tendency to structure experiences so that they provide meaningful satisfactions. Social roles are prescriptions for behavior that are shared by members of a social group. Social roles may arise to define relationships in the family, in the work setting, in educational settings, or in other social situations. Through our participation in social roles, we learn what others expect of us and we come to expect certain behaviors of others. Thus, some part of the regularity of thought, feeling, or action that we call "personality" is an expression of the kinds of social relationships in which one participates. The fourth component, coping style, is the person's preferred pattern of responding to challenge and stress: an important element of personality is the capacity to interpret unexpected, difficult, or unpleasant events in a way that preserves personal integrity and permits continued adaptation. These factors will be treated separately in the next four chapters.

The Life-Span Perspective on Personality Development

The life-span perspective challenges some assumptions and raises some questions about personality during all the phases of life. One strongly held view is that the major forces contributing to personality development occur during childhood. Other views emphasize adolescence as a critical period for the crystallization of personality. Finally, some theories argue that adulthood brings its own changes in personality. The life-span view questions whether any one phase of life is more important or more predictive of personality characteristics than any other. It emphasizes the need to evaluate evidence about stability and change in personality from one period of life to another. It also recognizes the need to evaluate the contributions of unique events associated with each life period. Are some life stages especially likely to make a vivid and persistent impact on personality? Or could one say that each life stage brings its own crises and opportunities, each having an equally great impact on personality? The life-span perspective opens the way to this kind of comparative approach to personality development.

The life-span approach also draws attention to patterned changes in environments that are encountered throughout life. One moves from the family of origin through a period of adolescence, when family ties may be loosened, to a family of procreation or perhaps to a return to the family of origin. One may move through a series of larger and more complex educational settings, or one may leave the school environment to begin one's working life. Work settings are virtually inaccessible until adolescence. At that point, there may be some introduction to the work role. Ordinarily, one does not begin an active socialization into the world of work until later adolescence or early adulthood. Then the typical phase of job search results in changing work settings and work activities relatively often until a suitable work role is established. Finally, toward the middle of later adulthood, one commonly leaves the structured work setting for the more personally defined activities of retirement.

At any point in these more or less predictable changes in environment, there is the chance for a new interaction between the stable components of personality and the expectations or demands of the setting. At any point, one may encounter a setting that values a talent that had formerly been devalued or one that devalues a talent that had formerly been valued. For example, a rebellious, antiauthoritarian style may lead to conflict and rejection in the high school environment but be viewed as heroic in the college setting. A person who desires privacy and refrains from frequent social interaction may find support for his or her preference during adolescence but may meet resistance to this quality in establishing a family of procreation. Qualities that make for a successful executive may make for a bored or depressed retiree. Settings are not equally supportive of all their participants.

Stability and Change in Personal Characteristics

One of the obvious questions raised by a life-span approach to personality development is the question of stability and change. The term *development* itself implies change. We assume that the potential exists for growth, redefinition, and reorientation of personality. However, our definition of personality clearly includes the concept of consistency. If people responded in a thoroughly unpredictable, random manner to each new event, the concept of personality would never have evolved. If all people responded in the same way, defined themselves and others in the same terms, and shared the same array of feelings, the study of personality would probably be much nearer completion than it is. Both variability and predictability are part of the reality of studying personality.

In trying to understand the dimensions of stability and change, we return to the four components of personality and assess their potential for continuity and modifiability. In the chapter on traits and talents, we pursue evidence about the stability of temperament, the role of talent in personality formation, and the pressures from the culture to inhibit or enhance particular personal competences. In the chapter on motivation, we discuss the importance of particular motives, including needs for mastery, affiliation, and power, at various phases of life. Once again, we raise the question of the persistence and change of motives across life stages. The discussion of social roles suggests that some degree of stability and change is built into every culture. People continue to participate in some long-term roles, and yet some of the prescriptions for these roles change with age. The theme of crisis and coping suggests that a person has a history of experience with life crises that contributes to the continuity of coping style. However, new competences, new sources of information, and new personal goals will modify one's coping orientation over life stages. In Chapter 6, we look at three powerful longitudinal studies of personality development to begin to integrate and evaluate this difficult question. Across the life histories of individuals, what aspects of personality can be seen as consistent or predictable and what aspects seem open to revision? Is change or stability the more dominant pattern? Perhaps we will find that individuals differ even on this basic dimension. In other words, we may conclude that some people are likely to retain a more consistent, stable personality across life stages while others are more likely to be engaged in a continuous process of reorientation or reorganization.

The question of stability and change in personality development has clear theoretical importance. A view of personality development must include some analysis of the process of growth, the degree of expected stability, and the extent to which various life phases are likely to be dominated by stability or change. The question of stability and change is also central to a personal concept of self. At every life stage, the person may anticipate a future period of stability or change. Preparation for stability will lead to a quite different orientation than preparation for change. Suppose one goes off to college expecting the coming years to be a continuation of the social, intellectual, and emotional orientation of early adolescence. With this set, one is likely to perceive the anxiety and depressions that are normally encountered as part of loosening bonds with parents, more intimate sexual experimentation, or strong pressures for career commitment as disruptive, even as signs of going crazy. If one begins this phase with an expectation that it will be a time of reorganization and change, then these same feelings can be interpreted as a form of normal developmental tension that will precede important growth. Knowing that we can rely on the relative stability of certain competences or coping strategies can provide reassurance during periods of crisis or change. Anticipating some periods as opportunities for growth can permit that growth to occur without the fear of abandoning familiar but inadequate personality characteristics.

Contribution of Culture to Personality Development

Cultural influences on personality are pervasive and continuous. We may perceive cultural influences as distinct, obvious pressures. For example, our culture expects children to be toilet-trained at about 2 years of age. In some African cultures, toilet training is achieved during the first year of life. In India, in contrast, peasant children are taught toilet habits by their peers, and few expectations are imposed during the first few years. These differences reflect broader cultural expectations about the importance of self-control, cleanliness, obedience to authority, and autonomy during infancy and early childhood.

Cultural influences may also have an impact through a more subtle communication of patterns or life rhythms. For example, child-rearing emphases on autonomy and independence begin with the decision for the infant to sleep in a separate bed, apart from the mother and father, and continue to be expressed in early expectations for self-feeding, hired babysitters to care for children, and school experiences away from the family beginning at age 3. These and other cultural expectations suggest that independence is a cultural value. It is viewed as a sign of maturity and is nurtured by important cultural institutions. Individuals who succeed in becoming independent benefit by the cultural value placed on this trait. Those who are more dependent or who find less satisfaction in independence will find fewer cultural supports for that style.

Culture has an impact on each of the factors of personality. Traits and talents may be valued or ignored by the culture. In a comparison of children from six cultures, Whiting and Whiting (1975) observed that cultures that were organized in nuclear families, in which parents and their offspring are the primary family grouping, tended to emphasize more sociable, intimate interactions. Cultures organized in extended family groupings, in which the generations of men and male children were separated from the generations of women and female children, tended to value and encourage more authoritarian, aggressive behavior. These cultural differences in family groupings would result in more reinforcement for sociability in some societies and more reinforcement for aggressiveness in others.

Individual traits and talents may be enhanced or inhibited depending on the extent to which sex-role norms are supportive of personal qualities. Societies that make sharp distinctions between male and female roles will limit the expression of "feminine" qualities in their males and the expression of "masculine" qualities in their females. Cultures that value collaboration and cooperation for survival will have strong sanctions against competitiveness. Cultures that value aggressiveness and individuality will have few reinforcements for a nurturant, empathic style.

The culture also influences the formation of motives. Depending on which needs are normally satisfied and which are normally frustrated, the culture can shape the importance of certain activities and goals. In our society, for example, status is associated with wealth and influence. In other cultures, status may be associated with having visions, attaining a certain age, or having the right ancestry. To the extent that status is achievable through one's own actions or accomplishments, the cultural determinants of status are relevant to the expression and satisfaction of motives.

Like traits and motives, roles are influenced by culture. Each society has its own age-related norms, differentiating the behavior expected of infants, young children, adolescents, adults, and the elderly. Cultures also differ in the variety of roles that are open to a person, the prescriptions for particular roles, and the interrelation among complementary role groups. In two African societies, for example, the grandmother is expected to take her grandchildren away from their parents and to care for them herself for several years after they are weaned (Stephens, 1963). This kind of expectation makes the grandparent role quite different from the grandparent role as it is defined in our society. It also changes the experiences young children have and their relationship to their parents. Finally, it changes the relationship between the parents' and grandparents' generations.

Finally, turning to coping styles, each culture has its own definition or implicit criteria for maturity or mental health. For example, Heath (1977) evaluated the 65 most and 65 least mature students nominated by other students and judges in American, Italian, and Turkish colleges. In all three cultural groups, the mature students were characterized as "purposeful, realistic, predictable, ordered, fulfilling potential, and clear thinking." Only the American judges picked mature students who were characterized by "enthusiasm, high energy level, and aggressiveness." This kind of comparison suggests that while there may be some commonality across cultures in shaping the direction of effective coping, there are also unique accents or emphases in what different cultures view as desirable. The extent to which deception, competition, cooperation, meditation, self-abasement, or hallucinating is viewed as an effective strategy for coping with crisis depends on the cultural orientation toward that strategy. The range of coping strategies will be limited by the cultural support that exists for these and other potential responses to stress.

Methods and Problems of Measurement in the Study of Personality

A variety of methods have been used to study personality development. Some methods reflect a particular theoretical position. Other methods are based on interpretations of carefully collected data (Fiske, 1978). Each method has strengths and limitations. Depending on the method used, investigators will focus on some set of behaviors at the expense of others. In this section, we describe five methods of study that are commonly used to understand the structure and development of personality.

Case Study

The case study is perhaps the most familiar strategy for studying personality. Freud's use of cases to illustrate the principles of his theory spawned a strong tradition of case analysis, especially in clinical psychology and psychiatry. Some classic case studies, such as *Lisa and David, Joey the Mechanical Boy*, or *The Three Faces of Eve*, provide a rich description of the fantasies, fears, and thought processes of severely disturbed patients. More contemporary cases, such as Erik Erikson's *Gandhi's Truth* or Nancy Friday's *My Mother, Myself*, offer a blend of the conflicts, fantasies, and adjustments that normal and outstanding people experience in dealing with the challenges of life. Many of these studies offer a psychohistorical perspective, integrating changes in the individual life history with currents of social and political change.

Case material can come from interviews, personal diaries or letters, therapy sessions, or prolonged observation. Contemporary case studies generally draw on a variety of methods, using interview responses as well as more structured assessment techniques to identify the dominant characteristics of the person. Robert White's *Study of Lives* (1963) offers an outstanding example of the case method applied to normal personality development. Using multiple methods, White has maintained contact with his subjects from later adolescence well into adulthood. He is able to blend retrospective data about the person's past with current evidence about life patterns, coping style, and personal characteristics to provide a rich picture of personality consolidation and change.

Projective Tests

The term *projective test* takes its meaning from the concept of *projection*, which Anna Freud (1936) identified as one of the basic defense mechanisms. Through projection, the person converts anxiety about undesirable impulses, conflict, or guilt into a fear of some external threat. The person is thereby able to disguise his or her own fears and focus attention on the danger from outside.

Projective tests are based on the assumption that direct questioning will not reveal many of the areas of conflict that are part of the personality—whether because the person deliberately conceals conflicts or thoughts that are seen as undesirable or because the person is not consciously aware of those conflicts. Projective tests bypass direct questioning and rely instead on the trained interpretation of symbols, stories, and imagery contained in the person's responses to ambiguous stimuli, such as inkblots.

The most famous projective tests are the Thematic Apperception Test (TAT) and the Rorschach Inkblot Test. Both tests invite the subject to make responses to ambiguous stimuli. In the TAT, subjects are shown a standard set of pictures. The pictures show males and females, adults and children in a variety of poses and moods. Each picture is vague enough to permit many interpretations. Subjects are asked to tell what is happening in the picture, what led up to this particular scene, and what will happen next. In the Rorschach, subjects are shown a standard set of inkblots. Some are black and white, some are in color, and others are black, white, and red. Subjects are asked to tell what they see in the blots. In both tests, interpretation of the responses is based on coding systems that have been

Figure 1–1. Rosenberg Self-Esteem Scale

1. On the whole I am satisfied with myself.
2. At times I think I am no good at all.
3. I feel that I have a number of good qualities.
4. I am able to do things as well as most other people.
5. I feel that I do not have much to be proud of.
6. I certainly feel useless at times.
7. I feel that I am a person of worth, at least on an equal plane with others.
8. I wish I could have more respect for myself.
9. All in all, I am inclined to feel that I am a failure.
10. I take a positive attitude toward myself.

Subjects rate each item on the scale below:

Strongly agree	Agree	Disagree	Strongly disagree

From *Society and the Adolescent Self-Image,* by M. Rosenberg. Copyright 1965 by Princeton University Press. Reprinted by permission of Princeton University Press.

developed to identify the motives or thoughts that are likely to generate each type of response.

Questionnaire Assessment

The questionnaire is a method that is commonly used in personality research. Questionnaires may involve self-reports, in which the person is asked to describe his or her own characteristics or feelings. An example of a self-report questionnaire is Rosenberg's self-esteem scale. Ten items (see Figure 1-1) provide a global measure of the person's overall feelings of self-worth.

Other personality assessment questionnaires make use of objective test items, including tests of intelligence, creativity, particular abilities, or attitudes. Questionnaire measures can be used singly or in combination. In theory building, Cattell (1957, 1973) has relied heavily on questionnaire measures to identify the general traits of personality. Cattell (1966) has described what he considers to be the more global dimensions, or source traits, that provide the integration and direction to personality. The main descriptive categories that have been derived from Cattell's work are listed in Table 1-1. These categories are based on questionnaire responses from a large number of subjects.

The kind of analysis Cattell used to identify personality traits from questionnaire data has several limitations. First, the categories that emerge depend on the kinds of questions that are included originally. Second, the blending of responses from many subjects in order to derive gen-

Table 1-1. Major Personality Factors Derived from Cattell's Work

Letter Symbol	Technical Title	Popular Label
A	Affectia–Sizia	Outgoing–reserved
B	Intelligence	More intelligent–less intelligent
C	Ego strength	Stable–emotional
E	Dominance–Submissiveness	Assertive–humble
F	Surgency–Desurgency	Happy-go-lucky–sober
G	Superego strength	Conscientious–expedient
H	Parmia–Threctia	Venturesome–shy
I	Premsia–Harria	Tender-minded–tough-minded
L	Protension–Alaxia	Suspicious–trusting
M	Autia–Praxernia	Imaginative–practical
N	Shrewdness–Artlessness	Shrewd–forthright
O	Guilt proneness–Assurance	Apprehensive–placid

From *Theories of Personality* (3rd Ed.), by C. S. Hall and G. Lindzey. Copyright 1978 by John Wiley & Sons, Inc. Reprinted by permission.

eral categories reduces the unique profiles of individuals to a group average. These statistically derived categories may not be accurate descriptions of the basic characteristics of individuals (Allport, 1937; Hall & Lindzey, 1978). However, questionnaire assessment does have the advantage of providing quantifiable data that are comparable across subjects or for a single subject across time. The validity of the categories derived from these data must be determined by relating them to behavioral observations that will confirm their accuracy.

Behavioral Observation

A look at Cattell's list of personality factors in Table 1–1 should make it clear that there is a problem in translating verbal labels of attributes into specific behaviors. Take, for example, the factor imaginative–practical. If a woman loses her door key and manages to open the door with a hairpin, is that imaginative or practical? If an older person on a fixed income starts a family babysitting service where senior citizens spend the weekend with children while their parents go away, is that imaginative or practical? If a young child who wants a toy that is out of reach gets the cat to jump up on the shelf and knock it down, is that imaginative or practical?

One way around this semantic problem is to base judgments about personality on the pattern of observable behaviors. This approach emphasizes the importance of linking attributes of personality to behaviors that do not require interpretation. Instead of looking for behavior that is friendly, aggressive, or dependent, one begins by recording such things as touching, smiling, hitting, or whining (Fiske, 1978; Jones, 1972). For example, Jones (1972) described the patterns of social interaction of preschool children during nursery-school free play. During 5-minute periods, the occurrence of 22 behaviors was coded for each child. Three factors emerged that described the children's play. Factor 1, which Jones called "rough and tumble" play, was based on the categories "laugh," "run," "jump," "hit at," and "wrestle" at one pole and "work" at the other pole. Factor 2, which Jones called "aggression," included the categories "fixate," "frown," "hit," "push," and "take-tug-grab." The third factor, called "social behavior," included the categories "point," "give," "receive," "talk," and "smile." Each factor reflects the common meaning or grouped occurrence of the behaviors it includes. An important distinction is made here between behaviors that can be understood as playful and those that can be understood as aggressive. Wrestling, for example, is a behavior that adults might label as aggressive. Yet in children's interactions, wrestling is more often a part of playfulness and less likely to be involved in a seriously angry or aggressive interaction. This type of analysis suggests that it is possible to talk about common groupings of behaviors that are expressions of an underlying form of social behavior. Individuals will all perform all of these behaviors at some time or another. By looking at the focus of activity for individual children, the frequency of each type of encounter, and the extent to which these various types of activities are directed toward peers, toward toys, or toward adults in the environment, we can begin to provide an analysis of individual differences that is based on patterns of observable behavior.

Experimentation

Experimentation is the method of research that psychology has borrowed most directly from the physical sciences. It is a method intended to determine whether one event or factor causes another. In an experiment, some variable or group of variables are systematically manipulated while others are held constant. Any change in the subjects' reactions is attributed to the manipulation (Rosenthal & Rosnow, 1975; Wuebben, Straits, & Schulman, 1974).

Let us look at an example of the experimental method in order to see how it is used to clarify the causal links between events. Seligman (1975) has suggested that an important element of mental health is the perception that one has control over life events, that there is some causal connection between one's responses and related outcomes. Long exposure to an uncontrollable environment can lead to depression, withdrawal, or psychosomatic ailments. Pennebaker, Burnam, Schaeffer, and Harper (1977) tested the hypothesis that lack of control over an environmental event would lead to increased reports of physical symptoms. Subjects sat in an experiment room wearing headphones. They were told they would hear a loud noise, which they could stop by pressing a button "the appropriate number of times." Each subject escaped from the noise 31 times. Half the subjects could stop the noise by pressing the button exactly five times. The other half had to press the button anywhere from one to nine times in order to stop the noise, the average number of presses equaling five.

After the experiment, the subjects completed a symptom checklist, rating the extent to which they had experienced 13 symptoms during the experiment. Although the subjects in the two conditions did not differ in their reports of frustration, alertness, or tension, the subjects in the "1–9 push" condition reported a greater degree of every physical symptom and a statistically greater degree of seven out of the 13 symptoms than those who could stop the noise with five pushes every time. This experiment does not explain the mechanism whereby lack of control increases sensitivity to symptoms. It does provide evidence for a causal connection between lack of control over an unpleasant stimulus and greater perception of physical symptoms.

Control is the key to successful experimentation. By "control" we mean the careful consideration of all variables that might influence the outcome of the study. Control must be exercised in selecting subjects to participate in the study. The subjects must bring comparable skills. We could not compare responses of subjects to written instructions if some could not read English and others could. Control must be used in presenting the task to the subjects so that such things as the instructions, the order of presentation, or the setting where the study is conducted do not interfere with the responses under study. We would not test some subjects in a noisy restaurant and others in a library unless the level of distraction was a variable under study. Finally, control is required in comparing the behavior of the subjects. After the experimental manipulation, subjects' behaviors are compared with their own behavior before the manipulation or with the behavior of another group of subjects who did not experience the manipulation. (This latter group is called the "control group.") If we did not have these kinds of comparisons, there would be no way of judging just how much the experimental manipulation mattered.

Regardless of the method of research, the study of personality is problematic. Here we will focus on four issues that are frequently raised in the evaluation of research on personality development. These are validity, stability and change, cohort or generational factors that influence personality, and situational factors.

Validity.   What does a particular instrument measure? This is the basic question of validity. A thermometer measures changes in temperature. A ruler measures distance in some standard units, such as inches or centimeters. But what about a test of intelligence or a test of masculinity and femininity? How can we be certain that a particular psychological instrument measures what it promises to measure?

There are several strategies that help with this problem. The most straightforward technique is to establish *face validity*. One simply evaluates whether the questions asked are appropriate to the topic. For example, if you are interested in measuring self-esteem, questions that ask people to rate how worthwhile they are have face validity. However, if you doubt whether people will really tell you that they are fantastic people even when they believe that, then you may doubt whether the response to such a question is a valid measure of self-esteem.

A second technique is to establish a *criterion group* that is expected to have the qualities that the instrument being developed is intended to measure. If you have a measure of anxiety, you might want to see how children who have a school phobia or people who bite their nails perform on this test. The performance of the criterion group will give some support to the adequacy or sensitivity of the measure. Of course, for some constructs the criterion group would be hard to identify. Whom would you select as a criterion group for a measure of independence or creativity or flexibility? Most likely your selection would depend on your own definition of the concept. To the extent that definitions differ, so will the selection of the criterion group.

A third approach to establishing validity is *convergent validity*. If an instrument is in agreement with other measures of the same dimension, then it is said to have convergent validity. Let us take the example of achievement motivation. This concept refers to the desire to achieve success when competing against a standard of excellence. Do subjects who score high on your measure of achievement motivation also do well in school; do they persist at difficult tasks; are they rated by teachers, supervisors, or peers as having a strong desire to achieve success; do they score in the expected direction on related measures of risk taking, fear of failure, or self-esteem?

The issue of validity is relevant for every measure and every method. It is as necessary to demonstrate the validity of an experimental manipulation as it is to demonstrate the validity of questionnaire items or projective tests. Does pushing a button to stop a noise really provide a sense of control over the environment? How can we be certain? Does a symptom checklist have any more validity than a story told in response to an ambiguous picture? Some measures have more apparent validity than others, but it is always important to try to evaluate just how close one's measure is to one's conceptual understanding of a process or an idea.

You can educate yourself about the problem of validity by spending some time with editions of Buro's *Mental Measurements Yearbook*. In this catalogue of psychological tests, instruments that have been used commercially, in research, or in clinical practice are briefly described and evaluated. Select a general topic, such as sex role, anxiety, creativity, or leadership. Then look up the variety of instruments that have been used to measure this concept. You will begin to appreciate a number of related issues. First, in psychological research there are many approaches to measuring the same concept. Second, the measures differ because the definition of the concept differs from one psychologist to another. Third, many tests are used in research and in practice even though their validity has not been established. This simply means that you, the reader, must try to impose your own appreciation of the concepts being measured on the results of the research. You must take an active role in trying to discern the range of applicability of the research you encounter, looking for areas of convergence with other studies in order to build your own system of relationships and truths.

Stability and change.   We have discussed the theme of stability and change as a major issue in a life-span treatment of personality. Here we would point out that it is also a basic question in the design and interpretation of research. Theories differ in their prediction of stability and change in personality. What is more, some theories conceive of repeated periods of temporary flux or crisis followed by reintegration and relative stability. One might expect, from this kind of analysis, to tap into phases of comparative organization or disorganization of personality, depending on when during the person's development one sampled. There is longitudinal evidence of children whose early life events would suggest an adulthood of competence and growth but who end up as adults feeling confused and despairing about their lives. In contrast, some children whose early-life events seem filled with conflict, disruption, and misfortune reach adulthood with a powerful sense of direction and vitality. And there are children and adults who report temporary periods of disorganization, only to rebound from these crises with resilience, having developed a creative strategy for coping with stress.

The research design will undoubtedly reflect the scientist's expectation about whether stability or change is more likely. In evaluating research data it is, once again, up to you to determine where in life's stream the ladle of observations has been dipped. Further, you must begin to look for evidence about whether the pattern that has been portrayed is likely to persist or to be redefined at some subsequent period.

Cohort factors in personality development. Every sample of subjects is drawn from a historical period and a generational cohort. A cohort is a group of people who were born at about the same time. Subjects who participate in studies of adolescent development in 1980 will have been born during the late 1960s. Those who participated in studies of adolescent development in 1960 were born during the late 1940s. Each cohort faces a slightly different future. Its members' education, the kind of parenting they are likely to have received, the quality of health care that was available, the orientation toward vocational development, and the prevailing cultural orientation toward childhood, adolescence, adulthood, or aging are all examples of generational features that may influence the direction of growth. In addition, historical events, including wars, famines, economic crises, political revolutions, and natural catastrophies, touch large groups of people during a particular period of their lives. These events call for adaptations that may dramatically alter the values or the life-style of a generation.

The question that is posed by these generational differences is how to appreciate them as separate from the more global mechanisms of personality change. For example, Levinson (1977; Levinson, Darrow, Klein, Levinson, & McKee, 1978) has reported on the major life transitions of 40 men who represented four professions. These men, who were in the age range 35–45 during the early 1970s, were born between 1925 and 1935. Among this group there appeared to be a major transition at about 28–33 between an exploratory phase during the twenties and a more established, "settling down" phase in the later thirties and forties. We might raise several cohort questions about this pattern. First, how much does the timing of "settling down" depend on one's anticipation of life expectancy? Will future generations feel less pressure of age? Finally, was the experience of conflict and crisis during the period 28–33 a product of the general cultural instability that was experienced during the 1960s, or is it a reflection of a predictable period of personality reorganization?

Situational factors. The issue of situational factors that influence personality requires both conceptual and methodological clarity. Our view of personality includes an emphasis on coping and adaptation. Clearly, each person must have strategies for responding to new situations or new circumstances. We do not expect people to behave the same at the office, at a party, in front of a large audience, and in private. The contribution of the context, however, is very difficult to establish. For example, we know that students who attend small high schools tend to be more involved in school activities and more committed to the school than students at larger schools (Barker & Gump, 1964). However, when students from small and large schools are compared for their involvement in college, the small-school students are no different from the large-school students. Involvement appears to be fostered by the setting; it does not become characteristic of the person's general orientation to new settings. However, Astin (1977) has traced the process of value change during the college years. The impact of smaller, single-sex, prestigious colleges seems to be the greatest in increasing the liberal attitudes of students. This increase in liberal orientation appears to persist well into adulthood, especially among those who marry partners with similar liberal views.

The question of the impact of environment on personality really involves *three* related questions. First, are some people more readily influenced by their settings than others? Second, are there times in one's life when the environment is especially likely to make an enduring contribution to personality? Third, does the impact of any single setting depend on the extent to which its contribution is strengthened or challenged by other settings? From a life-span orientation, we would be interested to see whether people select similar kinds of settings as they move through life. We would also want to know whether people have consistent styles of adapting to situational demands. We expect that most people will be somewhat flexible in adapting, insofar as they are able to read the obvious cues about sources of reinforcement or punishment, the avenues for success or failure that exist in each new environment.

Plan of the Chapters

Let us return to our working definition of personality as that relatively consistent set of thoughts, feelings, and behavior patterns that guide the organization of experience and the direction of new growth. The remaining chapters of this book are designed to clarify the basic components of personality and their interrelations.

Chapters 2–5 focus on the four components of personality: traits and talents, motivations, roles, and crisis and coping. In each of these chapters, the life-span perspective is maintained by emphasizing questions about stability and change and by identifying the contributions of each factor at various life stages. Chapter 6 presents data from three longitudinal studies of personality development. In each study, we have the opportunity to examine a unique approach to the definition and measurement of personality. Each study also provides a source of evidence about the important structures of personality and about the patterns of stability and change. Chapter 7 focuses on the self-concept and its relation to the concept of personality. In this final chapter, questions are raised about the experience of selfhood: what do we know about ourselves, how do we perceive ourselves, and in what ways does our self-understanding change over the life span?

Chapter Two

Temperament and Talents

One of the oldest and most persistent directions in the study of personality has been the effort to identify stable characteristics of the person that endure through time and across situations. The concepts of "trait," "type," "temperament," and "disposition" all reflect an approach that searches for the observable uniformities that can be used to group people together along some particular dimensions. This view of personality emphasizes that there are meaningful categories that can be applied in order to highlight the similarities among some people and their differences from others. For example, we might say that some people are more "outgoing" and others are more "reserved." This is not to say that all outgoing people are alike on all other traits, but rather to point out their similarities with respect to social encounters and, at the same time, to contrast them with people who have quite the opposite social orientation.

In addition to traits, this chapter also focuses on talent as a dynamic organizing component of personality. By "talent" we mean any of the enormous range of competences at which one might excel. It is a special sort of ability, such as athletic skill, musical skill, a good head for figures, or a flair for writing. A talent can be recognized by the relative ease with which competence is achieved and by the degree of pleasure normally associated with exercising the talent. Ideally one's talents can provide relatively conflict-free avenues for experiencing effectiveness and success.

The expression of any talent depends on the opportunities available for exercising that talent as well as the response of the culture to the particular area of skill. A person who lives in the desert, far from any ocean, may not recognize a potential talent as a surfer. A child who is skillful at climbing steep rocks or recognizing birdcalls may not find much recognition for those talents in an urban classroom.

The contribution of talent to personality is especially powerful when a particular area of expertise becomes the energizing focus for creativity and growth. Through the exercise of one's talents, the opportunity arises for unique performances, for achievement of excellence.

The Concept of Temperament

A number of theorists have proposed models of personality that include a system of personality types. Table 2-1 presents a number of systems of personality types. One of the most famous is Sheldon's (1942) physical typology, which associates particular temperamental characteristics with body types. Sheldon identified three basic body builds that he argued were linked to particular cognitive, affective, and interpersonal characteristics. The *endomorph,* or fat, rounded body type, was associated with "viscerotonia," or relaxation, affection, and love of physical comfort. The contrasting *ectomorph,* or fragile, linear, delicate body build, was associated with "cerebrotonia," or restraint, love of privacy, and self-consciousness. The third body type, the *mesomorph,* or muscular, rectangular physique, was linked to "somatotonia," an adventurous, active, and assertive personality.

In a more recent study (Hanley, 1971) using Sheldon's ratings for body build and a reputation test called the "Guess Who" test, junior high school boys were asked questions like "Guess who in your class would be shy in front of the class." The findings indicated support for Sheldon's description of the mesomorphic and ectomorphic body builds. Mesomorphic boys had reputations for being daring, being leaders, being good at games, and taking chances. Ectomorphic boys had reputations for being serious, unhappy, listless, unfriendly, and embarrassed before the class. There were no significant relations for endomorphic boys. These findings support Sheldon's idea that body build is related to observable behavior. However, it is still unknown whether the relation between body build and personality is due to genetic factors, physiological factors, or social-expectation factors.

Some theorists have identified types of personalities that differ in their styles of perceiving or organizing experience. Jaensch (1938), a German psychologist, hypothesized the antitype, or S-type, who tends to mix and integrate perceptions, and the J-type, who is more focused and analytic. These types, Jaensch argued, were linked to heredity and nationality. Witkin, Dyk, Faterson, Goodenough, and Karp (1962) typed people as field-dependent or field-independent. This dimension refers to the person's degree of dependence on environmental cues for interpreting experience. Some people are more able to isolate their experiences from the surrounding context, whereas others rely heavily on the context to give each experience its meaning.

Other psychologists have focused on emotional types. Jung hypothesized the extravert/introvert dimension as a basic temperamental

Table 2–1. Types of Personalities

Theorist	Typology	Explanation
	Body-Build Types	
Sheldon	Endomorph	Fat, rounded body build associated with relaxation, affection, and love of physical comfort (viscerotonia)
	Ectomorph	Fragile, linear, delicate body build associated with restraint, love of privacy, and self-consciousness (cerebrotonia)
	Mesomorph	Muscular, rectangular body build associated with adventure, action, and assertion (somatotonia)
	Types of Perceiving or Organizing Experiences	
Jaensch	Anti-type or S-type	Tends to mix and integrate perceptions
	J-type	Focused and analytic
Witkin	Field-independent	Able to isolate experiences from the surrounding context
	Field-dependent	Dependent on environmental cues for interpreting the meaning of experience
	Emotional Types Extravert/Introvert	
Jung	Extravert	Directing attention toward what is outside the self
Eysenck	Introvert	Turning inward; concentrating on oneself or one's inward life
Freud	Psychosexual Stages Oral Anal Phallic Genital	Each type reflects focus on a particular body zone and a characteristic mode of interaction.

quality of personality. This dimension has been researched by Eysenck (1967) and appears to be a recurrent theme in most efforts to assess personality. Freud's theory of psychosexual stages (Freud, 1933/1964) has been used as a basis for describing personality types as oral, anal, phallic, and genital. Each type reflects a tendency to focus on a particular body zone and related interpersonal characteristics as a means of achieving emotional satisfaction.

These examples of typologies describe ways that a cluster of traits or temperamental characteristics hang together as an organizing focus of the personality. They are caricatures of kinds of people rather than accurate descriptions of individuals' actual predispositions. In contrast, traits are more narrowly defined. Traits are characteristics that a person displays under a variety of conditions. Traits may be characteristics of perceiving the environment, responding to the environment, or initiating interaction with the environment. Traits are generally thought of as stable aspects of personality that can be used to describe a person in a variety of situations. When someone is described as friendly, hostile, or sensitive, the trait is thought to be characteristic of the person at home, at work, at the supermarket, or at a party.

Traits may be peculiar to a person, or they may be found in many people. One of the most important aspects of traits is that they provide predictable dimensions for knowing other people. A person's central traits give him substance and meaning in the eyes of others. We come to expect people to behave in ways that express their central traits. A good friend is valued for her understanding, her wit, or her assertiveness. These traits are relevant not only for the way the person interprets and responds to experience, but for the way that others know and appreciate her.

Stability and Mutability of Innate Characteristics during Childhood

The study of stable characteristics of personality begins in infancy with an analysis of temperament. *Temperament,* as Allport (1961, p. 34) defined it, refers to "characteristic phenomena of an individual's nature, including his susceptibility to emotional stimulation, his customary strength and speed of response, the quality of his prevailing mood, and all the peculiarities of fluctuation and intensity of mood, these being phenomena regarded as dependent on constitutional makeup, and therefore hereditary in origin."

In a longitudinal study of infant development, Thomas, Chess, and Birch (1970) rated 141 newborns on nine temperamental qualities: activity level, rhythmicity, approach/withdrawal, adaptability, intensity of reaction, threshold of responsiveness, quality of mood, distractibility, and attention span and persistence. On the basis of their ratings, they were able to identify three groups of babies, those who were "easy," those who were "slow to warm up," and those who were "difficult." These temperamental groupings could be recognized as early as the second or third month of life. Table 2-2 describes the three kinds of babies and shows the

Table 2–2.   Temperamental Characteristics of Infants

Type	Description	Percent of Total Sample
Easy	Positiveness in mood, regularity in bodily functions, a low or moderate intensity of reaction, adaptability, and a positive approach to, rather than withdrawal from, new situations.	40
Slow to warm up	Low activity level, tended to withdraw on their first exposure to new stimuli, were slow to adapt, were somewhat negative in mood, and responded to situations with a low intensity of reaction.	15
Difficult	Irregular bodily functions, were unusually intense in reactions, tended to withdraw in the face of new stimuli, were slow to adapt to changes in the environment, and were generally negative in mood.	10

Developed from Chess, S., & Thomas, A. Temperament in the normal infant. In J. C. Westman (Ed.). *Individual differences in children.* New York: Wiley-Interscience, 1973, pp. 83–104.

frequency of each. In a follow-up of the children over 10 years, the authors pointed out that the consequences of any particular temperament depended on the response of parents to the child's attributes (Chess & Thomas, 1973). For example, it was easier for "difficult" children to learn to accept change and to enjoy new experiences if they had parents who were patient and accepting rather than critical and intensely willful themselves. If they had parents who were impatient and rejecting, the difficult children could not learn to accept change or enjoy new experiences.

Few dimensions of infant temperament endure unaltered through childhood. Infant temperament sets a pattern for the kinds of caregiving behaviors that are most likely to be stimulated by the infants. It also determines what kinds of interactions both parents and infants are likely to enjoy. Each dimension of temperament may be positively or negatively valued, depending on the cultural meaning of each characteristic and the ways caregivers respond to it. Taken separately, none of these temperamental dimensions will necessarily impair adaptation.

Temperament serves as a gatekeeper to environmental input and to individual responsiveness. Buss and Plomin (1975) have suggested three ways in which a person's temperament can influence the responses of others. First, temperament sets the tone for interaction. People who are sociable and who enjoy interacting with others will communicate a different mood as they encounter strangers than will people who are more reserved. They are more likely to put the stranger at ease and to respond in a friendly manner. The reserved person will be more quiet, more wary, and more likely to make the stranger feel self-conscious. Second, temperamental differences will determine the kinds of behaviors a person will most probably initiate. Temperamentally active people will be more likely to initiate activities that will bring them into contact with a great variety of objects and people. Constant initiation means that others are more likely to be aware of the presence of active persons and more likely to interact with them. Third, each temperamental quality may reward or discourage the responses of others. If a parent feels rewarded by his or her child's level of emotionality and enjoys the child's frequent expressions of joy, anger, or anxiety, the parent is likely to repeat those behaviors that stimulate this expression of emotion. If, however, the parent is embarrassed or disgusted by overt emotional expressions, he or she is likely to punish those expressions or avoid situations that evoke them.

Because one's temperament provides these three means of influencing the environment—setting the tone, inviting interactions, and reinforcing or discouraging the responses of others—temperament is expressed not only in regularities in the person but in regularities in patterns of environmental responses as well. Of course, temperament cannot control the broad array of possible environment responses. Below, we discuss three ways the environment can modify temperament.

First, the temperament of parents, particularly their sociability, their activity level, and their emotionality, may influence the kinds of parenting techniques they use and the ways they respond to their children's behaviors. The active parent may be impatient with an inactive infant. The sociable parent may feel rejected by a reserved or withdrawn child (Buss & Plomin, 1975).

Second, role expectations may reinforce or discourage temperamental qualities. Kagan and Moss (1962), in their longitudinal study of personality development, argued that because the male sex role included expectations for aggressiveness, temperamentally aggressive males were likely to be reinforced for this characteristic. From early childhood through young adulthood there was a fairly consistent pattern for the expression of aggressiveness among males. Those who were highly aggressive in childhood continued to show this characteristic as adults. In contrast, aggressiveness was not a stable characteristic for females. Female children who were rated as aggressive during their early years were not likely to continue to display this characteristic as young adults. When major role expectations conflict with temperamental predispositions, the person is likely to suppress temperamental preferences to some extent in order to achieve social acceptability. The more narrowly defined a role is, the more it restricts the expression of certain aspects of individual temperament that people bring to their role enactments.

The third environmental factor shaping temperament is the cultural value placed on certain modes of interaction. Let us look, for example, at Turnbull's (1972) description of the Ik of Uganda as an extreme case of cultural adaptation. Forced into a terrain in which famine and crop failure are predictable every fourth year because of climatic conditions, the Ik are engaged in a culturewide struggle for survival. They are highly individualistic. Adults are concerned with their own ability to procure food. The young and the old are both neglected and taunted as the stronger adolescents and adults push for survival. Adults do not collaborate or pool their resources. When they find food, they eat it rapidly in order not to have to share with others. The Ik do not talk much to one another. They deliberately lie to one another. When one Ik stumbles or falls, the others laugh. One particularly amusing pastime is to watch a baby crawl toward the fire and touch its hand to the hot coals. When boys and girls play, their activity includes building houses and then wrecking the houses built by one another.

The fate of a child named Adupa in the Ik culture suggests the kind of conflict that is possible between the individual's temperamental predisposition and the cultural norms for social interaction.

> The best game of all, at this time, was teasing poor little Adupa. She was not so little—in fact, she should have been an adult, for she was nearly thirteen years old—but Adupa was a little mad. Or you might say she was the only sane one, depending on your point of view. Adupa did not go and jump on other people's play houses, and she lavished enormous care on hers and would curl up inside it, her distended stomach clasped in her sharp, long arms. That of course made it all the more jump-on-able, and Atum's nephew and granddaughter, Lokwam and Nialetcha, used to fight to be the first to jump. Lokwam was particularly vicious, and the other children usually let him have his own way, unless there were enough of them to beat him up. Then when Adupa pulled herself from the ruins of her house, crying, Lokwam became genial and let others join in as he beat her over the head and danced around her [Turnbull, 1972, p. 114].*

Adupa cared to do a good job and did not want to destroy the play houses of the other children. Since these qualities were not valued by the Ik, she was especially vulnerable to attacks by others in her culture. In the American culture, this example of conflict is comparable to the high school student who is not athletic or to the adult who is preoccupied with vivid, imaginative fantasies. The culture would view such behavior as maladaptive or as a sign of illness.

---

*From *The Mountain People,* by C. M. Turnbull. Copyright © 1972 by Colin M. Turnbull. (New York: Touchstone/Simon & Schuster, 1972.) Reprinted by permission of Simon & Schuster, a Division of Gulf & Western Corporation.

In summary, we can see temperament as producing certain repeated, stable environmental responses. At the same time, the environment can have a persistent impact that will modify temperament. The continuous interaction between temperamental predisposition and environmental regulation will most certainly be represented in the person's conceptualization of self.

Long-Term Resilience of Temperamental Characteristics

At the heart of the life-span approach to development is the question of just how stable personal characteristics are throughout life. As one might expect, the answer is complicated. In fact, the answer is not yet fully articulated. It depends on the variables being measured, the ages being studied, and the sex of the subjects. Let us describe some of the research findings that bear on the question of long-term stability of temperamental characteristics.

When we are looking for stability, we are most likely to find it over shorter rather than longer time spans. We are most likely to find stability in variables that have a direct physiological basis, such as heart rate or activity level, somewhat less likely to find stability in measures of intelligence, and least likely to find it in more global personality characteristics, such as dependency or self-confidence (Macfarlane, 1963). For example, Sontag (1966) reported on the stability of the heart rate during the fetal period and in adolescence. Subjects who showed high variability during the fetal period were also likely to have a variable heart rate at age 18. To the extent that heart-rate variability is linked to differences in levels of arousal or emotionality, we can begin to see the foundation for a view of temperamental stability.

Other work has focused on the social, or interpersonal, component of temperament. Bronson (1967) reported on a sample of subjects who had been studied from infancy until about age 30. The dimension of expressive/outgoing versus reserved/withdrawn was especially consistent for males from adolescence through adulthood. Expressive adolescent males were described as warm, self-accepting, and productive adults. Thus, expressiveness was not only a stable personal quality for males but a good predictor of other positive adult outcomes. For females, a consistent pattern of expressiveness was observed for one group but not for others. In this group, expressiveness was associated with adult ratings of assertiveness.

In the same study, another dimension, placid/controlled versus reactive/explosive, showed a very different pattern. For females, the rating of reactivity or control in the period from 11 to 13 was a consistent, stable predictor of adult style. This dimension was a good predictor of adult adjustment, especially characteristics of warmth, stability, openness, and responsibility. For males, there were three patterns: some males were consistent, some showed an increase in consistency during the adolescent and adult years, and some became less consistent from early childhood to adolescence. Whereas remaining consistently controlled was tied to adult productivity and some degree of constriction, a decline in control was associated with disruptive impulsiveness in adulthood. Here we have a pattern quite similar to that described by Kagan and Moss (1962), one interpersonal characteristic showing stability for females and quite a different one showing stability for males.

The sex differences in the stability of social orientation are most likely a product of the sex-role expectations and accompanying cultural socialization for males and females. Outgoingness is more likely to retain its stable contribution for males, whereas placidity and control are more persistent in the development of females.

Tuddenham (1959) reported on the stability of 53 personality characteristics in a longitudinal sample from adolescence to adulthood. These variables included such traits as introspection, creativity, animation, and social assurance. For the male sample, ten variables showed statistically significant stability. The strongest of these was drive aggression. For the female sample, nine variables were significantly stable, the strongest being social prestige. Variables showing little stability included physical attractiveness, self-confidence, and, for men, leadership and popularity. Tuddenham makes two important observations about his findings that deserve our consideration. First, a fairly large group of variables showed a positive correlation across the long interval from adolescence to adulthood. We can infer from this that the notion of long-term stability of personal characteristics is a valid concept. The second point, however, is that the magnitude of these correlations was low. In other words, on every variable measured it would be difficult to predict whether a particular person was more likely to remain the same or to change on that dimension.

The problem of prediction is addressed more directly in Macfarlane's (1963) observations about the Berkeley Guidance Study, conducted at the Institute of Human Development at the University of California, Berkeley. Macfarlane reported that when subjects were seen as adults, close to 50% were judged to be "more stable and effective" than had been predicted from observations made during childhood or adolescence. Here we are dealing not only with the question of a statistical prediction about the stability of a single temperamental characteristic but with the more global prediction of a person's adaptive capacity. Macfarlane suggests that experiences or circumstances that may appear stressful or even traumatic may turn out to be growth-producing. She also argues that early habits or patterns that appeared to be taking the person toward overdependence or isolation could be dropped or traded for new, more adaptive patterns. These changes did not occur without some confusion and anxiety. Yet, especially in adulthood, it appeared that many people were able to make use of new experiences or new roles to achieve the sense of personal and social maturity that they lacked during earlier phases of development. This is shown in the case of a subject who made passing grades and "who was a social isolate and a self-centered, unhappy boy . . . , now the manager of a large construction firm. He states that his primary satisfaction on the job is 'feeding graded doses of increasing responsibility and difficulty in assigned jobs to the work staff and watching them grow in confidence as their competencies increase' " (Macfarlane, 1971, p. 409).

These studies alert us to a special problem in a life-span approach to the study of personality. On the one hand, we are tempted to use our statistical information from one period of observations to predict the nature of future observations. Given a certain range of variability, we expect that future observations will be within some range of the average of our earlier findings. That is, we use the mean and variance of responses from time 1 to make a judgment about time 2. On the other hand, we know that there may be important intervening events that make a prediction of stability inappropriate. Changes in roles, changes in status, or the development of new competences may make earlier characteristics far more appropriate or far less appropriate at time 2 than they were at time 1. A stubborn, determined child, for example, may receive criticism or hostile responses from adults who expect compliance. As an adult, however, this same person may find that the personal characteristic of stubborn determination accounts for a variety of successes. Indeed, if it made sense to predict stability across the life span, the whole question of personality development would be superfluous. Why bother to study something that remains the same?

In fact, what we are searching for in the study of temperament is some clue about patterns of continuity. We are searching for themes that will offer an image of the person's most likely orientation. Is the person more likely to plunge ahead or to proceed with caution, to express feelings or to remain reserved, to seek diversity and novelty or to prefer what is already familiar? These kinds of predispositions provide a clue about how the person is likely to approach the range of life experiences that one confronts at each new stage of development. Although we would predict that these orientations will remain stable, we understand that they provide only a general sketch, or outline, of the personality. The finer details— that is, the array of individual traits and their implications for adaptation—appear to remain open for continual redefinition, refinement, and new learning.

Block (1971) has added to our understanding of the question of continuity or change in his analysis of longitudinal data from the Oakland

Growth Study and the Berkeley Guidance Study, both developed through the Institute of Human Development. The consistency of personality dimensions across three periods of life was examined: junior high, senior high, and adulthood. For both males and females, from junior to senior high, there was a strong consistency in personality dimensions. From senior high to adulthood, the consistency in personality dimensions decreased slightly. These findings once again suggest some basic continuities across life stages, with decreasing consistency across longer periods. What the findings disguise is the various patterns of change experienced by individuals in the sample. Among the males, for example, for 13 subjects there was almost no relation between ratings in senior high school and adulthood. Among the female sample, four subjects showed a tendency toward a negative relation between ratings in senior high and adulthood.

In order to understand the question of stability and change more fully, Block separated those subjects who tended to show a stable pattern from one period to another from those who tended to change from one period to another. Table 2-3 illustrates some of the differences observed (stated separately for males and females) between those who changed during the period from junior to senior high school and those who did not and also between those who changed from senior high school to adulthood and those who did not. These observations are drawn from data collected in adulthood.

> The Changers appear less adjusted during the adolescent years and particularly during the senior high school period displayed a marked neuroticism. However, they then manifested appreciable maturation and by the adult years the earlier differences ... appear to have vanished. There are certain strengths and certain weaknesses in the Changers as adults and there are different strengths and different weaknesses in the Nonchangers in the most recent interval during which they were assessed. In the average, they cannot now be distinguished but the qualities underlying these averages are still clearly visible [Block, 1971, p. 106].

From this analysis we realize that not only are some temperamental characteristics more stable than others, but some people have an earlier-crystallized personality structure, leading to greater continuity across life stages, than others. What is more, the tempo of growth or change is associated with different degrees of complexity, flexibility, and self-insight. Finally, the pattern of change appears to have different consequences for males and females. In general, for males, stability of personality is associated with greater social and moral maturity.

For females, the consequences of personality change are more diverse. Females who are observed to change from junior to senior high appear to be following what might be described as a normal pattern of personal maturation. In other words, for females, changes during the years

Table 2–3. Characteristics of Changers and Nonchangers

Period of Change	Changers		Nonchangers	
	Males	*Females*	*Males*	*Females*
Junior to Senior High School	Thin-skinned, fearful, brittle, self-defensive, overconcerned with own adequacy, compares self with others, uncomfortable with uncertainty, complicating of simple situations, reluctant to act, aloof, condescending, deceitful	Productive, turned to for advice, ethically consistent, physically attractive	Intellectual capacity, values intellectual matters, rapid tempo, insightful, introspective, arouses liking, socially poised, straightforward, gregarious, giving, physically attractive, interested in opposite sex	Moody, self-pitying, self-deceiving
Senior High School to Adulthood	Self-defensive, extra punitive, projective, undercontrolled, self-indulgent, irritable, bothered by demands, deceitful, fluctuating moods	Fantasizing, thinks unconventionally, initiates humor, sensuous, rebellious, married, contacts parents frequently, politically conservative, involved in politics, high family income, felt parents urged to high standards of conduct, would not consider financial security in evaluation of job possibility	Wide interests, verbally fluent, values intellectual matters, socially perceptive, incisive, ethically consistent, philosophically concerned, introspective, warm, calm, overcontrolled	Conservative, moralistic, conventional, self-defensive, high aspiration level

Adapted from Block, J. in collaboration with N. Haan, *Lives through Time.* Berkeley, Calif.: Bancroft Books, 1971.

from 11 or 12 to 15 or 16 reflect the normative pattern of personal development. Change from senior high to adulthood is more complex. Females who continue to modify basic elements of their personality after their high school years can be seen as moving in a less traditional, more highly differentiated direction. More than likely many of these women will begin to test out the limits of the female sex role in an effort to achieve a life-style more congruent with their unconventional orientation.

Talent

Earlier in the chapter we differentiated talents from temperament. Talent may be viewed as another potential source of continuity for personality development because it can provide an organizing focus for life activities. Think of people who like to work with their hands, people who excel in athletics, people who have musical ability, or people who have a "good head for figures." Each of these areas of competence offers an opportunity for experiencing effectiveness as well as avenues for social encounters, leisure activities, or career directions.

The study of talent has been pursued primarily with the goal of identifying and measuring particular aptitudes. For example, the search for successful Air Force pilots, submarine crewmen, or servicemen who would survive the Arctic climate led to the development of the methodology for assessing adult vocational aptitudes and to the emergence of a vast applied professional role of career guidance (Office of Strategic Services Assessment Staff, 1948). The kinds of talents that have captured the interest and energy of the scientific community have tended to be those related to intellectual and scientific activities, particularly studies of the intellectually or mathematically gifted (Keating, 1976; Nauman, 1974; Stanley, Keating, & Fox, 1974).

At Johns Hopkins, Julian Stanley has developed a program to study mathematically precocious children in the 12–14-year age range (Stanley, Keating, & Fox, 1974). The project involves identifying mathematically gifted children and developing their talents. For each student, some special program was developed to nurture his or her skills. Some attended accelerated courses, some enrolled in junior-college night classes, some attended university summer sessions, and some enrolled early in universities. One of the students in the program is Eric Jablow. He entered Brooklyn College after sixth grade and graduated *summa cum laude*. He won a National Science Foundation graduate fellowship to help support his graduate work at Princeton. At the age of 15, Eric will be Princeton's youngest doctoral candidate (Nevin, 1977).

One of the most impressive efforts to study the consequence of talent for lifelong development has been Terman's longitudinal study of exceptionally bright children (Terman & Oden, 1947, 1959). We will have more to say about Terman's study in Chapter 6. Here we will simply point out that Terman's data and subsequent observations of the same sample suggest that intellectual talent that was identified early in childhood has been associated with lifelong benefits, including good physical health, mental stability, and academic achievement. The intellectual resources of this group have provided them with the resilience and problem-solving skills that continue to foster successful adaptation throughout adult life (Kagan, 1964; Seagoe, 1975).

One area of talent that has special meaning for the study of personality is *creativity*. All through life, there are demands to make choices, to resolve conflict, and to identify personal priorities. In most of these situations, there is not one correct answer. Rather, successful adaptation reflects the person's ability to make an accurate assessment of both environmental resources and personal attributes relevant to the life plan. The emphasis on creativity as a personal talent reflects our interest in those unique solutions to life challenges that are part of many individuals' personal histories. Each of us knows a person who has taken a serious life upset and turned it into an advantage or who has set a course for personal growth that includes unconventional roles or an uncommon pattern of life activities. Creativity in this sense can be seen at many phases of life in the person's ability to impose a unique and growth-producing interpretation on life events.

The concept of creativity has been studied from many perspectives, not all equally applicable to the study of personality (Dellas & Gaier, 1970). One approach has been to equate creativity with the quality of the productions a person has created. For example, Albert (1975, p. 144) has offered the following definition of creative genius: "A person of genius is anyone who, regardless of other characteristics he may possess or have attributed to him, produces, over a long period of time, a large body of work that has a significant influence on many persons for many years." In this same line of thinking, Wallach (1976) has argued that real-life accomplishments during high school and college are more predictive of later attainments than grades or test scores. What is more, the range of attainment tends to be quite specific. A person who excels in theater is not necessarily going to create unusual science experiments or new mathematical models. Accordingly, in our effort to nurture creativity during an early life stage, it is important to link areas of individual talent to experience or programs in which skill in that talent will continue to be valued.

A second view of creativity focuses on the quality of thought that is involved in a creative response (Kogan & Pankove, 1972). Here we see an effort to differentiate between convergent thinking, or finding the single best answer, and divergent thinking, or finding many, varied, and unusual answers (Guilford, 1967; Kogan, 1973; Wallach, 1971). Of course, both kinds of thinking are part of normal cognitive functioning. Sometimes we search for the one best answer or solution to a problem. Often, however, we try to generate a list of the many possible explanations or options before selecting one.

In an attempt to differentiate between the adaptive capacities of highly intelligent and highly creative adolescents, Getzels and Jackson (1962) selected two groups of subjects from the population of a private Midwestern secondary school. The highly creative group scored in the top 20% on the creativity measures but below the top 20% on tests of intelligence. The highly intelligent group scored in the top 20% on tests of intelligence but below the top 20% on measures of creativity. Three comparisons between the two groups are of interest. First, both the highly intelligent and the highly creative groups earned higher grades in school than the average student population. Second, when teachers were asked to rate how much they would enjoy having each student in their class, the highly intelligent group received higher ratings than the creative group. Third, when the two groups were asked what kinds of occupations they would like to have, the creative group named more possible occupations and more "unconventional" occupations than the highly intelligent group.

Three implications can be drawn from these findings. First, intelligence and creativity are different. One person may be highly intelligent and highly creative; another may be highly intelligent but average in creativity; another may be average in intelligence and creativity. These two concepts provide different resources for adaptation. Intelligence is a resource used for memory, information processing, and analytic skills. Creativity is a resource used for originating novel solutions to problems and unique expressions of concepts in new forms.

Second, creativity appears to be a personal, inner resource that permits students who are not exceptionally intelligent to make highly effective responses in the academic setting (Walberg, 1971). Taylor (1975) has elaborated this component in an analysis of creative actions. He describes creative actions as those that bring aspects of the environment into line with the person's talents, motives, and inner experiences. In his model, creativity permits the person to modify or select elements of the environment, rather than be shaped by it.

Third, this research found that creative adolescents were not particularly highly valued in the student role. We can understand that creative students may resist coming to a final conclusion, they may offer more suggestions than the teacher has time to pursue, or they may ask questions that embarrass or perplex teachers (Torrance, 1970; Walberg, 1971). Torrance has described several aspects of the academic environment that inhibit the emergence of creative responses. They include the resistance that both teachers and students offer to divergent or unusual responses, the orientation toward success and external evaluation rather than achievement for its own sake, the conforming emphasis of peer pressure, and the cultural assumption that work is serious and productive but play is not. Within the pattern of developmental changes in creativity, Torrance finds that the seventh grade is one of the periods in the decline of creativity. At this entry point into adolescent development, the temporary increase in anxiety, academic expectations, peer pressures, and social roles all serve to decrease the nonevaluative approach to thinking that is conducive to divergent thinking (Torrance, 1962, 1965, 1975; Torrance & Meyers, 1970). One might well ask whether there are other socialization settings that discourage or inhibit creativity at other phases of life. To what extent do college courses, graduate education, work settings, family groups, professional organizations, or retirement communities foster novel, divergent responses from their participants? You might consider talking to people in professional organizations or retirement communities to find out ways their creativity is fostered or inhibited by those settings.

The study by Getzels and Jackson (1962) does not tell us about the adaptive resources or the social responses to adults and peers of students who are both highly intelligent and highly creative. These "creative geniuses" may in fact have special resources unlike those found in either the highly intelligent or the highly creative group. Additional research needs to be done to determine the adaptive responses of people who are both highly intelligent and highly creative.

The discussion of talent moves one rather quickly into the realization that talents may be either nurtured or ignored by the society. When one considers the diversity of skills that might be developed by any single person, it is clear that the waste of talent begins early in life. Many of the things children do easily (for example, dressing in "grown-up" clothes) are not seen as particularly important. But children who, by chance, are recognized for some culturally valued talent (such as playing the piano) may find themselves shuttled in a particular direction without much thought to the fit of that particular talent with other aspects of their personality, including temperament, motives, or intelligence. For example, a 5-year-old boy who can play a piano may have an active temperament that prevents him from sitting still for piano lessons.

It is important to recognize the great variety of talents that the great variety of human beings possess. In addition to providing the person with a sense of competence and self-definition, talents provide a diverse set of valued abilities for groups of people. Whether the group is the family, the town, the state, or the nation, one finds activities that are necessary in order to enhance group functioning. The fact that some individuals in the collectivity possess skills to accomplish these is important to the collective. The fact that the particular skills are important for the functioning of the group does not mean that every person needs to acquire the same set of skills; rather, the group recognizes individuals who have the relevant talents and allows them to emerge and to exercise their competences.

Talent, then, provides three rather special contributions to the total configuration of personality. First, talents offer an anxiety-free sphere for expressing competence. Each time a person uses a talent, the talent is used more easily, and the project is more likely to be done well. When a person does something well, the chances are that the product, as well as the activity, will be personally rewarding. Having even one sphere of special competence has the potential for producing experiences of mastery and efficacy that will encourage a general sense of well-being and decrease feelings of anxiety. Thus, the exercise and appreciation of one's talents result in a more generalized experience of personal enhancement and worth.

Second, particular talents can have social value. If one's talents are recognized as important to the functioning of the total community, they can become an avenue for more diverse roles, rewards, and status. Athletic talent, leadership ability, and entrepreneurial talents are examples of personal skills that can have expanding returns in personal growth in American culture. As these talents mature, they may become the focus around which new interactions, new challenges, and new expectations for achievement are encountered. Take, for example, the life experiences of an exceptional athlete like O. J. Simpson. Because athletic competence is highly valued in our culture, O.J.'s talents have been richly rewarded. As an athletic star, he not only has material rewards, but he is viewed as a hero by children, adolescents, and adults. His opinions and his life-style have far-reaching influences because of the admiration his special talents have produced.

Finally, well-developed talents may be the first line of response under conditions of crisis. When one is vulnerable or under attack, the responses that are most likely to surface as well integrated and resistant to stress are one's special talents. Of course, these well-practiced responses may not be appropriate for coping with emerging crises. It is, however, some comfort to know that certain areas of functioning can continue effectively even when one's energies are diverted by the intensity of unanticipated stress. Under some circumstances, one's talents may even offer the avenue through which conflict can be redefined to produce new opportunities for growth.

The following biographical material on the school experiences of Albert Einstein suggests something of the resilience of personal talents in the face of personal conflict and failure.

When Albert Einstein was fifteen, his father, Hermann Einstein, who operated a small electrochemical factory in Munich, Germany, failed in business and left for Milan, where he fancied business might be better. Hermann was a jovial, hopeful man, fond of beer and good food, of

Schiller and Heine. Albert's mother was an amateur musician, and the engineers from the factory often dropped in to hear his mother play Beethoven. Hermann's brother, another engineer, who lived with them, was an intellectual who was interested in politics.

In this home, which did not lack a love for learning and books and music, the boy they thought so dull was playing for hours on his own violin. He was reading Kant and other philosophers at eleven or twelve and such books as Buchner's *Force and Matter*. His speech was always hesitant; learning languages was difficult for him.

The family went to Milan when Einstein was fifteen, and he was left behind to complete his work at the Gymnasium in Munich; but he found school so intolerable that he asked the school doctor to give him a certificate saying he had a nervous breakdown and must spend at least six months with his parents in Italy.

It was at the formative age of sixteen that Einstein had a "time-out," a period of freedom from the classroom and scheduled activities. The warmth and beauty of Italy gave him complete satisfaction. He wandered through churches and hiked through the Apennines. It was at this time that he began to ponder what would happen if a ray of light were to be imprisoned—a query important to his later intellectual development.

In his upper-middle-class Jewish family there could be no tolerance for an idle boy who did not do well in school. Other relatives did better than Hermann Einstein, whose business in Milan was also unsuccessful; and it was they who gave a hundred Swiss francs a month to subsidize Albert, not out of faith but out of family charity, so that he might attend the Polytechnic Institute in Zurich, which took expatriate students. Albert had given up his German citizenship.

When he failed to pass his entrance examinations in zoology, botany and languages, there was nothing to do but go back to the secondary school and remedy his deficiencies. Einstein enrolled in an ordinary canton school in Arau, Switzerland, and after a year was admitted to the Polytechnic Institute in Zurich.

He once replied to a girl who wrote him a personal letter complaining about her teacher's not appreciating her: "I, too, was once treated so by my professors who did not like my spirit of independence and although they needed an assistant, refused to appoint me as one."

None of his schoolmates boasted of his friendship, and his teachers, when approached in later years, did not remember having had him in class. When he was graduated, he had difficulty in finding a position. He wanted to be a secondary school teacher but could not find a post. He answered newspaper advertisements, to no avail. He was a temporary assistant in a technical school for a few months; then he took a job tutoring slow students in a boarding school and was discharged because he insisted on teaching in his own way. He took a job in the patent office but kept on studying and publishing. As early as 1907 he presented material which was the main support for his theory of relativity, but it made not the slightest impression on the learned world.

In his autobiographical notes written at the age of sixty-seven Einstein said:

> It is, in fact, nothing short of a miracle that the modern methods of instruction have not yet entirely strangled the holy curiosity of inquiry; for this delicate little plant, aside from stimulation, stands mostly

in need of freedom; without this it goes to wreck and ruin without fail. It is a very grave mistake to think that the enjoyment of seeing and searching can be promoted by means of coercion and a sense of duty.

He disliked any artificial show of knowledge or learning of facts that cluttered up the mind. When asked about the speed of sound, he said that he did not know the answer to that question, but he knew where to find the fact in a reference book if and when he needed it. The important thing was to react delicately, and to have a perpetual sense of wonder [Goertzel & Goertzel, 1962, pp. 251–253].*

Chapter Three

Motivation

We can most simply describe motivation as the inclination to engage in some form of mental activity or observable behavior (Atkinson & Raynor, 1974). The inclination or motive is not itself observable. Instead, motives are inferred from the behaviors that are going on, the goal of those behaviors, and the events that alter the behavior (Birch, Atkinson, & Bongort, 1974; Murray, 1938). For example, if a baby becomes restless, starts making sucking movements, stuffs her fist in her mouth, gums the edge of her blanket, and eventually begins to cry, her mother may infer that the baby is hungry. If she offers a breast and the baby sucks eagerly, the mother will presume she was correct. After 15 minutes of nursing, if the baby begins to gaze around, coos and babbles, and shows little energy for nursing, the mother may assume that the baby is no longer hungry—in other words, that the motive has been satisfied. In identifying the motives that energize behavior, we continuously make hypotheses based on the direction, and changes in the direction, of behavior.

Three basic questions about motivation are addressed in this chapter. First, how do motives work to direct behavior? To answer that question we will examine three rather different theories that offer three views of the origin and function of human motives. We draw on the work of Freud, Maslow, and Allport to provide some intriguing contrasts to the analysis of motivation.

Second, does the importance of a motive change across the life span? This question, which seems central to an appreciation of a life-span approach, has not received extensive attention. We will look at the literature on four motives—mastery, achievement, affiliation, and power—with an eye out for evidence about the waxing or waning of these motives at various life stages.

Third, we are concerned about the contribution of culture to the expression of particular motives at different phases of life. We recognize that the acceptability of a motive, the intensity of the motive, and the particular way a motive is expressed in behavior are closely tied to characteristics of the environment. Motives are given connotative labels by the culture, they are linked to the availability of resources to satisfy the motive, and they are encouraged or discouraged through the expression of cultural norms. Think for a moment about the conflicts that arise around sexuality in our society. We tend to deny sexual motives among young children and to disapprove of pregnancy during adolescence, we encourage sexual experimentation in young adulthood, and we are skeptical about sexuality among the elderly. For each of these views, one could find a culture with quite the opposite emphasis. For example, in the Lepcha culture in South America, men view women as more sexually attractive and desirable after they have borne several children (Mead & Newton, 1967). In each society, one of the major goals of socialization is to encourage the person to want the same things for himself or herself that the larger social group wants and, at the same time, to encourage each person to reject or resist those impulses that are viewed as destructive to the social group. The manipulation of motives can be viewed as one of the primary tasks of the socialization process.

Three Theories of Motivation

We have selected three theories of motivation that are quite different in order to demonstrate how motives work to direct behavior. There are a great many theories of personality. Hall and Lindzey's (1978) classic text presents 15 theories, many of which draw on the works of more than one theorist. The purpose of this section is neither to review basic theories of personality nor to present a comprehensive summary of the role of motivation in every personality theory. The three views of motivation discussed below will help us examine the concept of motivation itself and its contribution to a life-span view of personality.

Freud's psychosexual theory focuses on the importance of two primary motivational systems that are present throughout life and operate within the limits of a fixed quantity of psychic energy. Maslow hypothesizes two levels of motives, one that operates in a developmental hierarchy and the other that is present at every phase of life to ensure continuous growth. Finally, Allport takes an extremely functional view of motives, looking at the contemporary goal of any behavior. In this view, motives can arise from biological, socioemotional, or cognitive sources. New motives can come into play at any stage of development. We will explain each of these three theories in detail, taking the opportunity to point out the implications of each for a life-span view of personality development.

Freud's Psychosexual Motives

The two motivational systems that Freud identified as having great impact on psychological functioning were sexuality and aggression, or, more broadly, the life instinct and the death instinct. Thus, not only are the motives or wishes seen to be in conflict with societal wishes, but they are in conflict with each other. The total quantity of psychic energy, or libido, fluctuates continuously between a thrust toward life and growth and a thrust toward death and destruction until the end of life, when psychic energy thrusts more toward death and destruction.

As Freud described it, the development of personality takes place in the context of a predictable pattern of changes in the focus of sexual and aggressive energy from one body zone to another. In this model, libidinal energy shifts from the mouth in infancy to the anus in toddlerhood to the genitals in early school age. At each stage of development, the new objects of sexual and aggressive satisfaction are expressed in new patterns of interpersonal relations and new forms of mental activity. The final stage of personality development occurs during adolescence. At this point, a convergence of biological and socioemotional maturation permits the total expression of sexual impulses in a heterosexual, loving relationship.

One of Freud's most significant contributions, and one that continues to generate controversy, is the importance he placed on the first six or seven years of life for the formation of personality. Freud (1905/1953) argued that from infancy children had strong sexual and aggressive impulses. At any one of the childhood stages, the child's efforts to gratify basic instincts could be so frustrated that the person would continue to seek gratification of those wishes at later life stages. Given that no person could possibly satisfy all his or her wishes and impulses at every life stage, Freud argued that for each of us there are important childhood origins to contemporary conflicts, anxieties, and personal habits. For example, if a baby's experience with sucking is so limited that her basic needs are not met, she will retain a strong need for oral activity later in life. Such a need may appear in the form of a habit such as smoking or talking too much.

Although the source of human motives may remain constantly bound to the sexual and aggressive instincts, the mode of impulse expression or satisfaction can change. For every impulse there are at least four avenues of expression—thought, symbolic thought, direct action, and symbolic action. For example, let us say that a young girl has a strong wish to be intimate with her father. She might think about lying in bed with her father, or she might imagine that she is a famous movie star and that lots of men are in love with her. She might go into the living room and cuddle up on her father's lap while he is watching television, or she might take a special gift to her male teacher at school. Depending on the person's age and the range of culturally acceptable behaviors, the person learns strategies for channeling impulses into activities or fantasies that are symbolic equivalents of those impulses. This process, which Freud called "sublimation," offers an array of changing avenues for the satisfaction of instincts. Of course, since sublimations are not direct expressions of the impulse, they are never fully satisfying. What is more, since the content of one's most profound wishes remains in the unconscious, inaccessible to conscious thought, one can never satisfy them fully without suffering some anxiety and guilt. Consequently, a pattern of arousal, expression, and inhibition becomes crystallized into a life orientation that will be recognized in episodes of gratification and frustration throughout adult life.

Maslow's Motive Hierarchy

Maslow's orientation to the study of personality focused on the creative potential of the person for growth. Maslow argued that in order to understand human potential it was necessary to study the experiences of healthy, even exceptional people. To this end, Maslow studied the lives of 49 prominent persons whom he considered to be examples of three groups: fairly sure cases of self-actualization, partial cases, and potential cases. Self-actualizing people are realistic, independent, creative, and democratic persons who have become everything they are capable of becoming (Nordby & Hall, 1974). In justifying his selection of these persons for intensive study, Maslow (1969, p. 726) says: "If we want to answer the question how tall can the human species grow, then obviously it is well to pick out the ones who are already tallest and study them. If we want to know how fast a human being can run, then it is no use to average out the speed of a 'good sample' of the population; it is better to collect Olympic gold medal winners and see how well they can do. If we want to know the possibilities for spiritual growth, value growth, or moral development in human beings, then I maintain that we can learn most by studying our most moral, ethical or saintly people."

In trying to conceptualize the forces toward self-actualization, Maslow proposed a model of motivation that has at its core an appreciation of the "fully functioning" person. Maslow believed that human beings are in a constant state of striving. There are few if any moments of total satisfaction or equilibrium. Rather, once one kind of need is satisfied, another emerges to direct behavior. Two motivational systems, describing two need concepts (deficit needs and metaneeds), exist in every person. The first group of needs, which Maslow called "deficit needs," includes physiological needs, safety needs, needs for belongingness and love, and esteem needs. These needs are critical for survival and for psychological health. They are viewed as emerging in a hierarchical order, so that physiological needs, including needs for food, oxygen, drink, and sleep, must be satisfied before focus will shift to safety needs, and so on (see Figure 3-1). Likewise, sudden disruption in the satisfaction of more basic needs will detract from the person's efforts to achieve satisfaction of needs that are higher in the hierarchy. For example, during a backpacking trip, one camper is lost in the wilderness for two weeks. He has water but no food supplies. As the days pass, he must search for food. This sudden disruption of the basic need for food will prevent the camper from satisfying needs that may have initiated the camping trip. He may have started on the trip to have adventure, to be close to nature, and to take risks—to satisfy self-actualization needs. Until the more basic needs are met, he will be unable to satisfy needs that are higher in the hierarchy.

Figure 3-1. A schematic representation of Maslow's need-hierarchy theory. (From *Personality,* by L. A. Hjelle and D. J. Ziegler. Copyright 1976 by McGraw-Hill, Inc. Reprinted by permission.)

At the top of the hierarchy are needs for self-actualization. These needs refer to efforts to realize one's potential to become everything one is capable of becoming. People who have reached self-actualization have satisfied their basic deficit needs. They can be described as knowing their place in life, having friends and loved ones, feeling a sense of belongingness, and having a sense of self-worth and self-respect. Self-actualizing persons are forward-looking individuals who can use their inner resources, such as temperament, talent, and motivation, to effectively adapt to life situations. Such people seem to have many characteristics that could classify them as "well-adjusted" people who have reached the top of the hierarchy in Figure 3-1.

You may be wondering what happens when people reach the top of the hierarchy: what motivates the person who has become self-actualizing? Once the basic deficit needs have been met, another need system, the metaneeds, emerges to direct the behavior of the self-actualizing person, who is then motivated by higher motivations, the metamotivations. The self-actualizing person has needs for unity, beauty, order, goodness, and justice. These needs play a significant part in fostering the person's continued growth.

> Gratification of the basic needs is not a sufficient condition for meta-motivation, although it may be a necessary precondition. I have individual subjects in whom apparent basic-need-gratification is compatible with 'existential neurosis,' meaninglessness, valuelessness, or the like. Meta-motivation now seems *not* to ensue automatically after basic-need-gratification. One must speak also of the additional variable of "defenses against metamotivation. . . ." This implies that, for the strategy of communication and of theory-building, it may turn out to be useful to add to the definition of the self-actualizing person, not only [a] that he be sufficiently free of illness, [b] that he be sufficiently gratified in his basic needs, and [c] that he be positively using his capacities, but also [d] that he be motivated by some values which he strives for or gropes for and to which he is loyal [Maslow, 1967b/1977, p. 29].*

The need hierarchy has clear developmental implications. If the needs must be satisfied sequentially, then one might assume that earlier life stages are more concerned with the physical, survival needs and that not until adolescence or even adulthood can one really begin to focus on the search for self-actualization or metaneeds. We might also infer that, in agreement with Freud's view of motivation, childhood is a precarious time for the gratification of basic needs. If a child has constant anxiety about meeting needs for food, safety, or love, then the chances of moving past those needs toward a state of self-actualization are less. However, Maslow suggests that if one can maintain a level of satisfaction with regard to basic needs, then there is the promise of further growth. The search for meaning, for the articulation of values, and for the achievement of creative forms of action draws people toward a life of continuous personal enhancement.

Two criticisms of Maslow's view of motivation alert us to the lack of specificity about which motives have priority. To put it another way, how literally can we take the concept of a hierarchy of needs? First, we know that prominent adults have emerged successfully from a childhood of adversity (Goertzel & Goertzel, 1962). The lives of James Baldwin, Viktor Frankl, and Sarah Bernhardt instruct us that relative deprivation in physiological, safety, or belongingness needs may not prevent the emer-

*From "A Theory of Metamotivation: The Biological Rooting of the Value-Life," by A. H. Maslow. In H. M. Chiang and A. H. Maslow (Eds.), *The Healthy Personality: Readings* (2nd Ed.). © 1977 by Litton Educational Publishing, Inc. Reprinted by permission of D. Van Nostrand Company.

gence of talent or the pursuit of self-actualization (Maddi, 1976). In contrast, there are examples of people who relinquish basic needs in order to achieve what they believe to be higher levels of awareness or fulfillment. Thoreau's retreat to the woods, Gandhi's fasts, or a firefighter's heroic rescue is evidence of a willingness to sacrifice more-basic needs for higher ones. Thus, although Maslow's model articulates an essential optimism about growth that appears to be lacking in the Freudian system, it still falls short of a satisfying analysis of the ways in which motives achieve priority in orienting human behavior.

Allport's Theory of the Functional Autonomy of Motives

At the center of Allport's theory of personality is the self, which he calls the "proprium" (Allport, 1955, 1968). Allport defines the proprium as "the self-as-known—that which is experienced as warm and central, as of importance" (1968b, p. 4). As such, the proprium gives uniqueness and integration to the personality. It is viewed as a developing entity that has seven identifiable functions, which emerge from infancy through adolescence. The seven propriate functions are these (Allport, 1955):

1. The sense of bodily self—all forms of body sensations.
2. The sense of self-identity—the awareness of the permanence of the self with recognizable boundaries and features.
3. The sense of self-esteem or pride—a personal evaluation.
4. The sense of self-extension—things that belong to or are associated with the self.
5. The self-image—how one is viewed by others; expectations others hold for one's behavior.
6. The self as a rational coper—the realization that one has problem-solving capacities and an ability for self-reflection.
7. Propriate striving—a capacity to formulate long-range goals, to direct one's life toward defined objectives.

The implication of this kind of definition of the self is to emphasize the forward-moving nature of human beings. People set goals, they make choices, they analyze their situations, and they influence the outcome of their own development. These processes are viewed as conscious, rational, and purposive. They are not bound to a reservoir of unconscious impulses or infantile motives that limit the range of potential areas for satisfaction and growth.

Embedded in this view of the person is Allport's conception of motivation. Allport has identified what he believes to be four requirements of a theory of motivation. First, the theory must account for motives as they exist in the ongoing, present experiences of the person. A motive must be operating to guide the contemporary array of behaviors in order to have meaning for the person. Second, a theory of motivation must recognize a variety of motives. Third, the person's own cognitive coping strategies must be included as having motivational properties. In other words, the theory must recognize that our aspirations can direct our behavior. Fourth, a theory of motivation must allow for similar motives to function in unique ways in different people. For example, the need for success may be expressed in private achievements, in a search for public acclaim, or in a commitment to the growth and accomplishments of one's children. All these criteria combine to express Allport's view of the person as one who is forward-moving and unique. Allport's emphasis on individuality as a crucial element in the study of personality is thoroughly embedded in his formulations about motivation:

> Now it is certainly true that we often wish to use universal and group norms. We want to know whether Bill, relative to others, is high or low in intelligence, in dominance, in affiliativeness. But although Bill can be compared profitably on many dimensions with the average human being or with his cultural group, still he himself weaves all these attributes into a unique idiomatic system. His personality does not contain three systems, but only one. Whatever individuality is, it is not the residual ragbag left over after general dimensions have been exhausted. The *organization* of Bill's life is first, last, and all the time, the primary fact of his human nature [Allport, 1968a, pp. 87–88].

The concept that Allport offers to express this contemporaneous, individualized, forward-looking view of motivation is the *functional autonomy of motives*. With this term, Allport is asserting that "a given activity may become an end or goal in itself in spite of the fact that it was originally engaged in for some other reason" (1961, p. 227). Thus, even if aspirations or goals began in the service of biological or survival needs, those needs do not necessarily continue to be the energizing forces behind the behavior. A person may initially perform a behavior because of some deficit need. For example, a person may take a job in order to earn enough money to support a family. Over time the behavior itself becomes pleasurable and valued, irrespective of its link to the original need. The person begins to enjoy the work and to value it for its own sake. The valued behavior, in this case work, becomes a functionally autonomous motive. The person will engage in work because of the satisfactions it brings. In an extreme example, the person may refuse a higher-paying job because of the pride and commitment that are already associated with the ongoing work activities. The situation might also be reversed. The person works because of a need to earn money in order to support a family. The person becomes good at making money and finds the process pleasurable. The pursuit of wealth becomes a functionally autonomous motive, taking priority over commitments to any particular job and, perhaps, even to the family. Thus propriate strivings or the motives for self-fulfillment can be unique to each person and constantly changing as the person's aspirations or life goals change.

As the example above illustrates, the concept of the functional autonomy of motives suggests that the motive base is flexible and open to change. Further, the same behavior may be directed by different motives in two persons. For example, two persons may become doctors specializing in cardiology. One person pursues this specialized area of medicine because of a need for power and prestige. The other has a need to help people. Likewise, similar motives may be expressed in quite different behaviors. Two persons may have a need to help others, but one becomes a cardiac specialist and the other a teacher of young children. In Allport's view, one could say that during adulthood it is the cognitive capacity to plan and to value that dictates the nature of one's motives.

Comparison of the Three Theories

In contrasting the three views of motivation, three observations can be made. First, the three views differ in the degree of stability they attribute to motives through the life span. At one end of the continuum, Freud has identified a narrow range of motives, the life instincts and the death instincts, that energize behavior continually throughout life. Maslow takes an intermediate position, describing a developmental hierarchy of needs that emerge during childhood, adolescence, and adulthood. Given a history of relative gratification, one can expect the behavior of adults to be a response to quite different motives than the behavior of infants and young children. Allport suggests a continually revised motivational base that is the product of values, aspirations, and transactions with the environment. His theory would argue that not only are adults different from children in their primary needs, but each person has a unique motivational history.

Second, a contrast often drawn among the theories has been between Freud's drive-reduction, or deficit, model and Maslow and Allport's growth-oriented, or humanistic, orientations. This comparison focuses on the homeostatic emphasis of Freud's theory as contrasted to the expansion orientation of the others. In Freud's view, motives press for satisfaction through fantasy, direct action, or symbolic expression. Once a drive is expressed, its intensity subsides until a new build-up of tension occurs. The two drives, tied as they are to biological survival, are never fully satisfied. Rather, they go through continuous cycles of tension build-up, expression, and tension reduction. Maslow and Allport both recognize that some motives operate according to this drive-reduction model. However, they both suggest that some motives do not have equilibrium, or homeostasis, as their goal. Rather, these motives move one toward an optimum state of stimulation, complexity, activity, or social involvement. They propel people to add dimensions of variability or uncertainty to their lives in order to grow.

We would only point out that the focus on growth is not entirely absent from Freud's model. In fact, the life instinct is just such a motive—an urge toward growth. Much of what Freud described was the areas of conflict and frustration that prevented the full expression of the life instinct. Although Freud believed the death instinct affected motivation, it would be accurate to conclude that all three theories acknowledge the existence of an intrinsic, organic commitment to growth. It can be inferred, since none of the theories suggests the contrary, that this growth orientation continues throughout adulthood. It not only is present during periods of physical maturation but is assumed to be a stable part of the person's adaptive capacities.

A third area of comparison is the relative emphasis on the biological, emotional, and cognitive components of motivation. Although no theory disregards these three sources of motivation, each view clearly emphasizes a different domain. Allport has the most cognitive orientation. His notion of propriate striving includes an appreciation of the motivating properties of personal plans, values, and goals. Maslow is most concerned with an emotional source of motives. Feelings of belongingness, self-esteem, and self-actualization can all be considered affective states that guide behavior. Although the metaneeds may be understood as more cognitively complex needs for understanding or meaning, self-actualization is understood mainly as a state of being, a desirable emotional condition. Freud's view is most clearly biological. Sexuality and aggression are defined as biological instincts inherited through membership in the species and expressed from infancy through the id, or pleasure-seeking function. Even before the person is capable of investing feelings in others or of thinking realistically about the physical or social environment, the libido exists to energize behavior. Libido is bound up with the biological reality of existence and owes no particular allegiance to the realm of feeling or thought.

We recognize the three sources of motives—the cognitive, the emotional, and the biological—as legitimate origins of behavior. We are a long way from being able to identify which of these factors has primacy during the various phases of adult life, but it would be unduly narrow to assume that one source of motives operated to the exclusion of the others. Undoubtedly some behaviors are energized by one primary motive base and others by all three.

Importance of Four Motives during Different Phases of Life

The focus of this section is on the waxing and waning of particular motives at various life stages. This approach allows us to examine the question whether a person's motive base changes with development. The literature on particular motives also takes us a step away from the theoretical formulations about how motives operate, toward a more functional analysis of the expression of concrete needs. Four motives—mastery, achievement, affiliation, and power—are discussed because each one highlights a unique component of the person's total coping capacities. An understanding of coping capacities, or active efforts to resolve stress, is important because it may provide an explanation of the behaviors that promote development and growth.

Mastery

Probably the most influential statement about mastery, or competence, motivation was offered by Robert White (1959) in his essay "Motivation Reconsidered: The Concept of Competence." The thrust of his argument is that an important source of energy that organizes or focuses behavior is the person's need to produce an effect on the environment and, eventually, to exercise mastery over environmental challenges. The competence motive shares the properties of the growth motives or propriate strivings discussed by Maslow and Allport. It is defined as a force toward effective action that is rewarded by the inherent feelings of pleasure associated with successful action. In White's view, this motive toward competence explains much of the perseverance and striving that a drive-reduction model of motivation cannot explain. Infants insist on feeding themselves even though they get less food into their mouths than would get there if someone fed them. Early-school-age children insist on learning to ride a two-wheel bicycle even though it would be easier to stick with a tricycle. Adults seek positions with administrative responsibility even though they would have less conflict and pressure in a more subordinate job. Older adults struggle to keep their own home or apartment rather than move into a senior citizens' home where services would be provided for them. Although each example concerns other motives in addition to competence motivation, each emphasizes the person's desire to exercise and retain feelings of competence rather than maintain the status quo or surrender control to others. In effect, White (1974) has argued that stability, or equilibrium, is not really a viable human alternative. Either we grow or we regress. Experience and challenge demand new expertise and new conceptualization. The implication is that the competence motive remains as a potent push toward growth as long as novelty and diversity are encountered.

Harter (1978) has elaborated on White's notion of competence, adding some important developmental implications. First, she differentiates two forms of competence motivation. One is a striving to overcome or master challenges, and the other is a striving to encounter challenges.

Second, competence strivings can be tied to several spheres of functioning, including the physical, social, and emotional domains. At every life stage one would not necessarily expect the person to focus on the same areas of concern. In infancy, for example, sensorimotor competence, the ability to incorporate and modify environmental stimuli, may provide the greatest source of satisfaction. In later adolescence, certain kinds of cognitive competences are essential for the formation of a personal identity; accordingly, we might expect cognitive achievements to be the focus of most strivings for competence.

Third, the intrinsic pleasure derived from success at mastery of a challenge can also be influenced by the attitudes of socialization agents, such as parents, toward competence. If parents do not approve of a child's action, they may reprimand the child even if the act was performed out of a striving for competence. For example, a 4-year-old child striving to be independent tries to cut his meat with a sharp knife. His father thinks his son is too young to use sharp utensils. The father abruptly grabs the knife away from his son and angrily tells him to ask Mommy or Daddy for help. What is more, if dependence or helplessness is viewed as desirable, a child's efforts toward mastery may be generally devalued. As Figure 3-2 illustrates, there are socialization factors that may decrease as well as increase the strength of the motive for mastery. In fact, Harter suggests that particularly during the early-school-age period there is some tendency to focus more closely on the approval or disapproval of adults for feelings of satisfaction in one's work than on the outcome of the effort per se.

In a study by Meid (described in Harter, 1978) children at two age levels, 6 and 10, were exposed to one of three levels of success—high, medium, or low. At each success level, children heard one of three kinds of adult responses to their performance: praise, no comment, or mild negative comment. These two factors, success itself and adult response, were viewed as possible contributors to the child's own evaluation of task performance and to his or her expectations for success on a future task. For the 6-year-olds, the child's evaluation and expectations were based heavily on the adult's response, not on the actual level of success. For the 10-year-olds, the child's evaluation and expectations were based on both the level of success and the adult's response. The 10-year-olds were able to identify their own success at the task as a separate component of a sense of mastery even though adult responses continued to influence their expectations about future achievement. Thus, the competence motive is vulnerable to the person's socialization history. In fact, one might assume that although a basic attitude toward competence and a delight in experiences of mastery are established during the middle school years, significant manipulations of the environmental reward structure could interfere with that motive at any point during adult life. Basically, however, we would expect that an early history of support of efforts toward competence and mastery would leave the person with a strong inner drive for such achievements without the need for continued external approval.

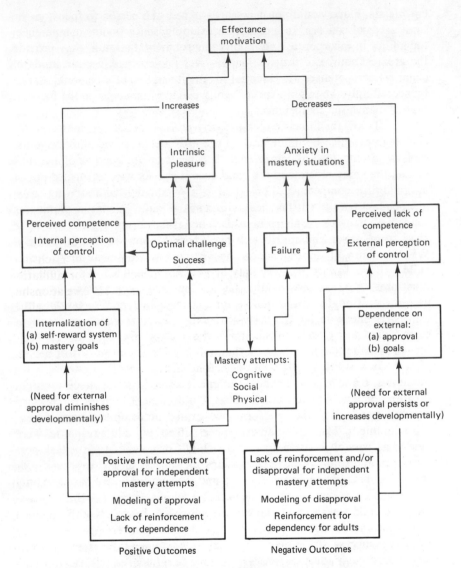

Figure 3–2. Developmental model of effectance motivation. (From "Effective Motivation Reconsidered: Toward a Developmental Model," by S. Harter, *Human Development,* 1978, *21*(1), 34–64. Reprinted by permission of S. Karger AG, Basel, Switzerland.)

Achievement Motivation

The conceptual framework for achievement motivation was initially advanced by Henry Murray in *Explorations in Personality* (1938). The need for achievement is the internal state of arousal that leads to vigorous, persistent, goal-directed behavior when a person is asked to perform a task, in relation to some standard of excellence (which may be defined by the person or by others), and where performance will be evaluated in terms of success or failure (Atkinson & Birch, 1978; Atkinson & Raynor, 1974). As this definition suggests, achievement motivation is not aroused in every situation. It is a meaningful motivational construct only when certain situational factors exist. There are also individual differences in the strength of the achievement motive.

The classic device for measuring achievement motivation, the Thematic Apperception Test (TAT), was developed by Christiana Morgan with Murray (Morgan & Murray, 1935). Murray discussed the human personality in terms of a variety of psychological needs, which were organized differently from person to person. Some of the needs Murray discussed are affiliation, achievement, dominance, autonomy, nurturance, and aggression. Although all the needs he described are present in all human beings, not every need is equally strong in each person. Each need motivates behavior. For example, if one has a high need for affiliation, one will do things in order to seek out others and to have relationships with others. If one has a high need for dominance, one's behavior will be directed toward gaining control of one's environment and of the people who are in it. The person who has a high need for affiliation and relatively little need for dominance will behave differently from the person who has a high need for dominance and relatively little need for affiliation A person who has a high need for both affiliation and dominance will behave differently still.

It can be seen that with a large number of needs, a wide variety of individual differences in motivation are possible, according to Murray's theory. In essence, Murray's conceptualization of personality suggests the development of a motivational profile for each person in order to understand that person's behavior. This type of analysis would run into difficulty if it did not also consider the environment in which the person behaves. Murray theorized that the arousal of needs was sometimes the result of conditions within the person and sometimes the result of situational conditions. For Murray, then, the motivational profile would have to include the demands of the situation that the person faces as well as the dominant needs that characterize the person. Thus, the person who is characterized by a strong need to achieve success would be highly motivated in any setting where standards of success and failure were clearly defined and where a demand was made for excellence (such as a school). On the one hand, if a contest were conducted for essay writing and a prize were given for the best essay, a student with high achievement motivation, a strong personal need to achieve success, would be motivated to try very hard to win the contest. On the other hand, if a student with high achievement motivation were just told to collect information about a topic for an essay, that there would be no right or wrong answer, no special reward for excellence, we would not expect this student to be highly motivated.

To the conception of the motivational profile, then, we must add a conception of the situation. According to Murray, in order to understand a person's behavior one must assess the fit or lack of fit between the person's motivational structure and the situational demands the person faces. In this section, we will be looking at the origins of the need to achieve success and at the behavior that characterizes people who are high or low in achievement motivation under different environmental conditions.

The origins of individual differences in achievement motivation have been linked to parental child-rearing practices. Winterbottom (1958) conducted a study with 29 8–10-year-old boys. She obtained a rating of each boy's need for achievement by asking him to tell stories in response to verbal stimuli that she presented. These verbal stimuli were similar to the TAT pictures we described in Chapter 1 in that they were vague enough to permit many different kinds of responses. The stories the boys told were coded for the presence of themes that would suggest the arousal of the achievement motive. If a story included a reference to a unique accomplishment, such as inventing something or solving a problem, that would be scored as achievement imagery. Other kinds of achievement imagery are references to the excitement or joy of sharing an idea or achieving a lifelong goal.

Winterbottom also interviewed the mothers of the boys in her sample, asking them to recall certain components of their child-rearing practices. Mothers of boys who scored high and who scored low on the need-for-achievement measures made equal demands for independence and mastery. However, the mothers of the high group tended to make earlier demands (before age 8) for many behaviors, whereas the mothers of the low group made their demands later (after age 8). Mothers of the high group tended to use more intense rewards for the fulfillment of expectations, particularly more physical signs of affection. Mothers of the high group also tended to evaluate their sons' behavior more positively than mothers of the low group.

In another study of the relation between achievement motivation and child rearing, Rosen and D'Andrade (1959) visited 40 families in their homes. Twenty of the families had a son aged 9–11 who had been identified as high in the motive to achieve success, and 20 had a son aged 9–11 who had been identified as low in the motive to achieve success. The experimenters watched each boy and his parents perform five tasks that required interaction between the child and the adults. The verbal communications and nonverbal help were coded with special attention to the extent to which parents expected self-reliance, the degree of autonomy parents permitted in decision making, and the kind and amount of emotionality introduced into the problem-solving situations. The findings of this study suggest that parents of boys who have a high need for achievement actually give their children achievement training. They set up higher standards of excellence, expect greater competence, and communicate greater approval after success than parents of boys who have a low need for achievement. Parents of the high group also differ in their response to the boys. Mothers tend to emphasize achievement by both encouraging and punishing in response to the quality of the boys' performance. The fathers of boys in the high group tend to allow the boys more independence, valuing self-reliance and mastery. Hence, the boy who shows a strong need for achievement is likely to have learned from his father the independence that allows the development of competence and from his mother the goals or standards of excellence that direct his behavior.

In general, the child-rearing environment of children who show strong achievement motivation includes early and continuing encouragement for achievement, a permissive orientation toward exploration and investigation, and reward or praise for achievement efforts (Smith, 1969; Stein & Bailey, 1973). In addition to child-rearing practices, the presence of role models who show children how things are done or who express satisfaction in experiencing competence or excellence helps children establish a personal motive for achieving success. Consequently, particularly for females, the desire to achieve success may conflict with a lack of models for how women express their needs in achievement situations (Darley, 1976; Hoffman & Nye, 1974; Zellman, 1976). The presence of male and female models who have high achievement aspirations in literature, in television programs, in visible community leadership roles, and, of course, in the family group will contribute to the internalization of strong motives and the expression of achievement-related behaviors.

Ollendick and Gruen (1971) conducted a study in which they found that third-grade children who were high in achievement motivation were better able to delay gratification (postpone receiving a reward or having a pleasurable experience) and to search for a higher level of solution to a learning task than third-grade children who were low in achievement motivation.

These studies show that there are identifiable differences in achievement-motivation behaviors among children during middle school age and that these differences can be used to predict differences in standards of excellence that children will strive for and differences in how long children will persist at achievement-oriented activities.

Research has also suggested that the need for achievement is a relatively stable characteristic of personality. Longitudinal studies have shown a consistent relation between the levels of achievement motivation at age 8 and age 14 (Feld, 1967; Kagan & Moss, 1959).

Imposed on this picture of motivational stability, however, is some indication of a developmental change in the perception of various situations that require an achievement orientation. For example, young children (under 5) tend to be equally impressed by success regardless of the difficulty of the task, whereas older children (10–12) are sensitive to the amount of effort expended in order to achieve (Nicholls [described in Weiner, 1978]; Weiner, 1978). In adulthood, it appears that task outcome may again become the more dominant factor in evaluating the achievement activity (Weiner & Peter, 1973).

By taking a cognitive approach, we can hypothesize what developmental changes might be occurring in the understanding of achievement orientation over the life span. Young children may be impressed by success regardless of the difficulty of the task because they lack an appreciation of intentionality. They are unable to understand the underlying motives and can see only the outcome—success or lack of success. Older children can appreciate a person's intention to succeed, independent of the consequences. They would be more impressed by a person who tried very hard but made small gains than by one who tried very little but made large gains. In adulthood, especially in work settings, the rewards of success are based on productivity. No matter how hard people try, if they do not meet the criteria imposed by the situation, the effort expended in the task may not be valued. This is not to say that adults do not understand the relation between intentionality and success. It is just that if the effort is not productive, the task outcome may not be valued.

The situation itself plays an important part in determining whether the achievement motive will be aroused. The achievement motive is aroused in situations that demand competition against a standard of excellence, where there is a strong emphasis on the importance of high-quality performance, and where there are psychological penalties for failure. The achievement motive is not aroused under more relaxed conditions, when there is little emphasis on criteria for performance (McClelland, Atkinson, Clark, & Lowell, 1953).

Once this finding about the interaction between situational components and motivational states was discovered, many experiments were designed to demonstrate the relation between achievement motivation and performance under varying environmental conditions. As the theory of achievement motivation was expanded and developed (Atkinson & Birch, 1978), additional motives that were aroused in achievement-oriented situations were discussed. The notions of fear of failure (Atkinson & Birch, 1978) and fear of success (Horner, 1968, 1970, 1972; Monahan, Kuhn, & Shaver, 1974) were introduced. It was assumed that in a situation where the possibility of success was emphasized, the possibility of failure was also present. It was also assumed that some people are motivated mainly by a need to achieve success and others are motivated mainly by a need to avoid failure. It was later discovered that a situation that emphasizes success could, for some people, also arouse a fear of success. Horner used the notion of fear of success in conjunction with the notion of the need to achieve in order to understand the behavior of women in achievement-oriented situations. Recent analyses have suggested that the motive to avoid success is present in both men and women. Actual fear of succeeding is conscious in some situations and not in others. Sex-role attitudes about "what a man shoud do" and "what a woman should do" will arouse anxious feelings for many individuals, depending on the situation. We might expect that some men would feel very uncomfortable about winning recognition for being interpersonally sensitive and empathic. Similarly, women might feel anxious about being recognized for their determination and assertiveness. The motive to avoid success may be as closely tied to one's ambivalence about the value or meaning of success as to sex-role stereotypes about male or female achievement activities (Condry & Dyer, 1976; Tresemer, 1977).

Affiliation and the Social Motive

One of the strongest advocates of a motivational force toward social involvement was Alfred Adler (1939/1964), a psychoanalyst. The following statement expresses Adler's conviction about the centrality of the social motive to human growth.

> It is almost impossible to exaggerate the value of an increase in social feeling. The mind improves, for intelligence is a communal function. The feeling of worth and value is heightened, giving courage and an optimistic view, and there is a sense of acquiescence in the common advantages and drawbacks of our lot. The individual feels at home in life and feels his existence to be worthwhile just so far as he is useful to others and is overcoming common instead of private feelings of inferiority. Not only the ethical nature, but the right attitude in aesthetics, the best understanding of the beautiful and the ugly will always be founded upon the truest social feeling [Adler, 1964, p. 79].

The social motive appears to have both a positive, action-prompting component and a negative, withdrawal-prompting component. Millham and Jacobson (1978) refer to these two sides of the affiliative motive as the hope of affiliation and the fear of rejection. The social motive may be aroused under conditions that promise to satisfy the hope or threaten to realize the fear. In fact, much of the research on the need for affiliation and the need for approval emphasizes the latter component—fear of rejection. For example, Atkinson, Heyns, and Veroff (1954) measured the strength of affiliative imagery after asking college fraternity members to rate one another in a group situation. The content of that imagery reflected a greater need to protect against rejection than a desire for more contact. Similarly, instruments designed to measure the need for approval, including Edwards' Social Desirability Scale (Edwards, 1957) and the

Marlowe-Crowne Scale (Crowne & Marlowe, 1960), reflect both the anxieties people have about the possibility of social rejection and the tendency to deny or avoid behaviors that may be perceived as undesirable.

In contrast to the motives that reflect a fear of social rejection, there is considerable behavioral evidence about the satisfactions of social interaction. From infancy, we are prepared to participate in social encounters. One of the earliest stimuli to evoke an infant's smile is the sound of the human voice (Wolff, 1963). Infants respond with interest to the visual array of the human face. They are able to differentiate some of the phonetic distinctions of human language. In interactions with animate objects, they engage in cycles of responsiveness and calm that suggest a capacity for rhythmic, reciprocal communication. In all these behaviors we recognize the competences and the intrinsic satisfactions that are part of normal social interactions.

Taking the need for social involvement a step further, another psychoanalyst, Sullivan (1953), has hypothesized the central focus on a need for intimacy and a dread of social isolation. As both psychodynamic and cognitive theorists have pointed out, the quality of social involvements changes as the person develops more mature cognitive capacities. As the notion of the self changes and as its characteristics change, so do the kinds of commitments that one can make to others. As children develop a greater understanding of the diversity of perspectives, they can be more responsive toward someone whose needs are not identical to their own. During adolescence sexuality and the desire for physical intimacy become important components of certain social interactions. At this point, there may be conflict between efforts to gratify social needs for understanding, affection, and approval and efforts to satisfy sexual needs for physical intimacy. Especially in early adolescence, it is difficult to bring these two kinds of social intimacy into harmony in a single relationship.

One of the best-developed views about a developmental shift in the social motive has been the disengagement theory of adaptation to aging offered by Cumming and Henry (1961). They argue that because death is an inevitable end, it is to the benefit of both the individual and the society for older adults to gradually disengage from social roles and withdraw from social interaction. This process of disengagement—that is, of dissolving investments in social relationships—would make death easier for the older person to accept and less disruptive for others.

Disengagement theory argues that older people who are less invested in their social community, their social relationships, and their social responsibilities will experience higher morale than those who continue to remain involved with their social milieu. Several factors contribute to the gradual diminution of the life space, including retirement, widowhood, the departure of children from the home, and the death of peers. These events stimulate a perception of a limited social context, which is responded to by a gradual loss of involvement in these and other relationships. Cumming and Henry describe the aging process as one of increased ego-centrism, including a dominance of personal motives, increased expressivity, and declining concern with reality.

A number of social scientists have offered evidence and theory in opposition to the concept of disengagement. Four criticisms of the theory are discussed below.

First, there is evidence that disengagement represents not a new adaptation during later life but a continuation of a life-style. Maddox (1968), in a discussion of activity level and life satisfaction among the elderly, has suggested that people who are high or low in activity generally maintain that ranking through repeated observations. People who displayed the disengagement pattern—that is, high satisfaction and low activity—were the very oldest ones. Maddox points out that they may have arrived at that pattern through several paths, not just as an adaptation to old age.

A second criticism is that older adults who are engaged in their social environment experience greater satisfaction than those who are not. Havighurst, Neugarten, and Tobin (1968) reported an analysis of Cumming and Henry's sample after seven years. This sample consisted of one cohort aged 50–70 in 1956, when the first interviews were conducted, and another cohort aged 70–90 in 1958, when they joined the study. Havighurst et al. attempted to differentiate between social engagement and psychological engagement. The former concerns activity in daily interactions and in life roles. The latter concerns a personal investment in relationships and a readiness to engage the complexities of social reality. Both these dimensions were found to decrease with age. This finding supports the disengagement process. However, measures of life satisfaction and emotional attitude toward social activity showed that those who were most active were most satisfied with life and those who were least active were least satisfied. There was no decrease in life satisfaction with age, but a strong expression of regret over the loss of role activity. Thus, older subjects were able to accept their current loss of activity, though with some dissatisfaction, and still maintain their overall self-esteem. These data point out the strong value that older adults place on social interaction and role activity. The fact that they can adapt to a decrease in activity does not mean that they wish it, only that they can cope with it.

A third criticism of the disengagement theory is that disengagement may reflect a current condition rather than a psychological necessity (Rose, 1968). Many of the cultural conditions that now force elderly people into a more restricted social environment are likely to change. As life expectancy increases, people in good health will be unwilling to limit their activities severely (Hamlin, 1977). Increases in economic security through Social Security legislation will provide the financial resources for continuing participation in social events. New forms of engagement, particularly the political identity of the older adult and interest in cultural, scientific, and artistic hobbies, will replace work as an involving role. All these opportunities for the elderly will encourage adults to redirect, rather than disengage, their energy.

The fourth criticism of disengagement theory rests in the evidence that the ability to maintain an intimate relationship with another person during later adulthood is an important source of self-esteem. In a study of 280 adults aged 60 and older, Lowenthal and Haven (1968) reported that the ability to have a close relationship with a peer is significantly related to the maintenance of high morale, positive psychiatric status, and an absence of depression. Part of the satisfaction of such an intimate relationship most likely derives from the values, experiences, and knowledge shared between the two intimates (Gamer, Thomas, & Kendall, 1975). Particularly when the adult encounters widowhood, friends become an essential component for life satisfaction (Flanagan, 1978).

An important component of some such intimate relationships may well be the sexual intimacy that is experienced. Masters and Johnson (1968) have provided a convincing argument that satisfying erotic experiences continue to be possible for 70- and 80-year-olds. Despite the capacity for sexual satisfaction and the feelings of intimacy it brings, older adults are confronted by social realities that discourage sexual expression. First, adults tend to think of later adulthood as a time when sexual interests vanish. Jokes about sex in old age, shocked glances at an older man and a younger woman, and admonishments from adult children suggest that sex is off limits for older adults (de Beauvoir, 1972; Rubin, 1968). Second, women are faced with the great likelihood that they will lose their husbands and still have their later adult years ahead of them. An older woman becomes a "sexual castoff," with few opportunities to reestablish the kind of intimate relationship that will provide sexual satisfaction (Angelino, 1977; Datan & Rodeheaver, 1977). The most significant factor for the continuation of sexual satisfaction is the opportunity to maintain sexual activity. Thus, the continuity of an intimate relationship, particularly a heterosexual relationship, can be seen to play a central role in the maintenance of a positive self-attitude.

In summary, we see the motive for affiliation and social involvement as one that retains its vigor throughout life. Periods of withdrawal or reserve may occur, particularly during times when feelings of vulnerability or uncertainty are high. Over the life span, however, we see evidence of powerful social motives beginning in infancy and continuing through later adulthood. Although these motives remain vigorous, the culture does not always provide avenues for their gratification. Thus, the themes of adolescent alienation, young-adult isolation, and later-adult disengagement emerge to alert us to the difficulties involved in developing reciprocal, mutually gratifying interpersonal bonds that meet needs for understanding as well as intimacy.

The Power Motive

The power motive has been defined as "concern over controlling the means of influencing the behavior of another person" (Veroff, 1957) or as a desire for "establishing, maintaining, or restoring power—that is, impact, control or influence over another person, group, or the world at large" (Winter & Stewart, 1978). As with achievement motivation, the Thematic Apperception Test has been one of the most frequently used devices to measure the power motive (Stewart & Winter, 1976; Winter, 1973). The stories subjects tell are coded for the extent to which images refer to actions that express power, images that arouse a strong positive or negative emotion in another person, or images that express a concern about reputation or position. Fear of power (a fear of being controlled) can also be coded when the story suggests that power is used for the benefit of another person, when the person has doubts about the ability to influence others, or when power is described as deceptive or ironic. In such stories, power is associated with distrust or ambivalence.

People clearly differ in the strength of the power motive and the fear of power. Characteristics that have been identified as correlates of the power motive include running for important student elections and holding important organizational positions; career choices as business executive, teacher, psychologist, clergyman, and journalist; seeking visibility through publicity; building a broad network of associates; participation in competitive sports; and a preference for certain prestigious belongings, including stereos, certain makes of cars, or a large number of credit cards (Winter & Stewart, 1978).

The power motive among males has been associated with a conflicted, exploitative orientation toward women. Men with a high motive for power tend to report earlier and more extensive sexual relations with women and to prefer wives who are dependent (McClelland, 1975; Winter, 1973). They are more likely to be involved in unstable marriages or to experience dissatisfaction in dating (McClelland, Davis, Kalin, & Wanner, 1972; Stewart & Rubin, 1976). The power motive is associated with similar career aspirations in females and in males. In females, however, it does not have the same association with disruption or instability of intimate relationships. One might expect that females who have a strong power motive and a nontraditional sex-role definition would resist the kind of heterosexual relationship in which they were expected to play out the dependent, submissive role.

Fear of power derives from anxiety about helplessness and early experiences of having been manipulated or robbed of autonomy (Erikson,

1950; Winter & Stewart, 1978). For males and females who have a strong fear of power, actions are directed toward preserving freedom and avoiding social relationships that might limit independence. Power situations tend to arouse a high level of anxiety, which may result in flight or disorganized behavior. Over time, the negative consequences of these situations tend to alert people to preserve their autonomy by avoiding structured situations, denying the influence of others, or ignoring rules or regulations that appear to infringe on personal freedom. One can expect that, over time, the strength of the power motive and the fear of power would direct quite varied life patterns. Individuals who have a strong power motive and a strong fear of power will behave differently in control-influence situations than individuals who are strong on one of the motives only.

Given that individuals may differ widely in the strength of their power needs, there is some evidence that the power motive undergoes something of a metamorphosis during later adulthood. Using the TAT pictures as stimuli, Gutmann (1969, 1974, 1975) provides cross-cultural data in support of what he calls a "massive transcultural involution" in the power needs of males and females. By "involution" he means the following.

> By contrast with younger men, older men are on the whole less aggressive. They are more affiliative, more interested in love than in conquest or power, more interested in community than in agency. The younger men see energy within themselves, as a potential threat that has to be contained and deployed to productive purposes. But the old men see energy as outside of themselves, lodged in capricious secular or supernatural authorities. For older men, then, power must be manipulated and controlled in its external form through postures of prayer and other forms of supplication and accommodation [Gutmann, 1975, p. 171].

In contrast to this pattern from greater to lesser sense of agency for aging men, Gutmann describes women as becoming more aggressive, more domineering, and more likely to assume an authoritative role in the family group with age. The basis for this transition, as Gutmann views it, is the lessening of demands from the parental role that have imposed a long period of sex-role differentiation and division of labor. As parental involvement declines, both males and females are freer to expand into the domains that had been established as areas of primary functioning and responsibility for the opposite sex. Of course, the less clear-cut these distinctions are during early adulthood, the less dramatic the redefinition or redistribution of power during the later years. We might also suggest that although the parent role may require a division of labor, participation in the world of work plays another strong role in stimulating the power motive. As males and females become equally involved in work activities, the picture of an age-graded reversal in the expression of power needs for males and females is likely to become less readily identifiable.

Impact of Culture on Motivation

The point to be made in this final section is, perhaps, so obvious that it bears no elaboration. To live in a cultural context is indeed to live in a psychosocial environment of expectations, resources, incentives, and sanctions that shape the predominant motivational profile of the group as a whole. The culture begins its contribution to motivation in the norms it prescribes for feeding, weaning, toilet training, bathing, and stimulating infants. We recall Erikson's (1950) vivid description of the Sioux mother's generosity in offering her breast on demand not only to her own child but to any hungry child. Role prescriptions associated with age, sex, occupation, or rank reflect a pattern of cultural values that shape the strength and the enactment of motives throughout life. The predominance of this cultural influence depends on the homogeneity or heterogeneity of the culture. Most probably, it is the particular subculture in which one is born that is most involved in the early socialization experiences of childhood. One's desires for achievement through success in school, one's ability to express affiliative needs, one's hope for or fear of power are initially shaped by the expectations and resources of one's immediate subcultural group. As an example, think of the implications for motivation of the following comments by a 56-year-old jobless miner from the Cumberland Plateau of eastern Kentucky who spoke with sociologist Harry Caudill.

"But I kept my young 'uns in school anyway. I come back home here to the mountains and raised me a big garden ever year and worked at anything I could find to do. I sold my old car fer seventy-five dollars and I sold all the land my daddy left me and spent the money on my children. They didn't have much to eat or wear, but they at least didn't miss no school. Well, finally last spring my oldest boy finished up high school and got his diploma. I managed to get twenty-five dollars together and give it to him and he went off to git him a job. He had good grades in school and I figured he'd get him a job easy. He went out to California where he's got some kinfolks and went to a factory where they was hirin' men. The sign said all the work hands had to be under thirty-five years of age and be high-school graduates. Well, this company wouldn't recognize his diploma because it was from a Kentucky school. They said a high-school diploma from Kentucky, Arkansas, and Mississippi just showed a man had done about the same as ten years in school in any other state. But they agreed to give the boy a test to see how much he knowed and he failed it flatter than a flitter. They turned him down and he got a job workin' in a laundry. He jist barely makes enough money to pay his way but hit's better than settin' around back here.

"I reckon they just ain't no future for people like us. Me and my wife ain't got nothin' and don't know nothin' hardly. We've spent everything we've got to try to learn our young-'uns something so they would have a better chance in the world, and now they don't know nothin' either!"*

* From Harry M. Caudill, *Night Comes to the Cumberlands: A Biography of a Depressed Area*. Boston: Little, Brown, 1962, pp. 337–338.

The hopes of this father are similar to the hopes of many middle-class American parents. Unfortunately, the resources of his community and the isolation of his subculture make the realization of those hopes almost impossible. Across generations, the socialization process will adapt to this reality by modifying the aspirations of parents and by imposing alternative values and rewards. In the example above, the family was overcome with helplessness. Other adaptations might include organizing the community to have influence on the school, robbing a bank to pay for expenses, withdrawing one's children from school to get jobs, or developing a personalized education system in one's home to meet children's individualized needs.

As a final example, we draw on Edgerton's (1965) comparison of values, attitudes, and personality characteristics expressed among the farmers and herders of four East African tribes. The assumption was that the work demands of these two occupational roles, with their accompanying patterns of daily activities, hazards, and social interactions, would generate distinct psychological profiles. The following differences between these groups were observed:

> Some of the confirmed expectations are relatively obvious—such as the fact that the farmers did indeed define wealth in terms of land whereas the herders did not. Others were more impressive: as we expected, the farmers divine and consult one another, the herders act individually; the farmers do value hard work, the herders do not; the farmers are indeed relatively more hostile and suspicious of their fellows than the herders. Some confirmed differences even extended as far as personality; e.g., the farmers tend to be indirect, abstract, given to fantasy, more anxious, less able to deal with their emotions, and less able to control their impulses. The herders, on the contrary, are direct, open, bound to reality, and their emotions, though constricted, are under control. It is apparent that even the crude analysis points to meaningful and predictable differentials between farmers and herders [p. 446].*

Although we recognize the existence of individual differences in the motivational profiles of members of a subcultural group, we would also argue that certain subcultural requirements impose motivational priorities on group members. The more isolated the subculture, the less aware a member is likely to be that his or her personal motives and goals are not shared by other groups. The process of development during adulthood entails gradual exposure to people from other groups, who have experienced different patterns of socialization. As a result of this contact, adults have the opportunity to identify the idiosyncratic nature of their own motives and to make deliberate choices about the investment of energy in alternative goals.

* From " 'Cultural' vs. 'Ecological' Factors in the Expression of Values, Attitudes, and Personality Characteristics," by R. B. Edgerton, *American Anthropologist,* 1965, *67,* 442–447. Reprinted by permission of the American Anthropological Association.

Chapter Four

Roles

In this chapter we move away from the inner space of the person that is reflected in such concepts as temperament, talent, and motivation to the enactment of social roles. A role can be defined as any set of behaviors which has some socially agreed-upon function and for which there exists an accepted code of norms (Biddle & Thomas, 1966; Brown, 1965). We are children, parents, teachers, students, friends, workers, citizens, competitors, and lovers. These and other roles refer to particular positions that exist in the society. Learning how to assume these positions, aspiring to enact certain roles, and feeling pressure from others for adequate role performance make an impact on the consolidation of personality. Especially roles that endure across many life stages, including the roles of child, parent, and worker, carry certain norms for behavior that will be integrated into a personal conception of self. What is more, the acquisition of new roles is generally accompanied by internalized expectations, or values, about how particular roles ought to be played. Not only do we come to define ourselves in terms of the primary roles we hold, but through the process of role enactment we internalize expectations for our own behavior and the behavior of others that shape subsequent interactions.

The Concept of Social Role

The concept of social role comes directly from the theater and the idea of playing parts in a drama (Sarbin & Allen, 1968). The parts exist independent of the particular actors who hold the roles. Similarly, social roles are components of social systems. They may be held by different people at different times. Of course, just as individual actors bring their own interpretation to the parts they play, so each of us brings his or her own unique talents, temperament, and motives to the interpretation and enactment of life roles. The concept of social role offers a framework for discussing the interaction between the person and the social environment. Through participation in various roles, people are at once shaped by the demands of those positions and contributors to the subsequent definition of those roles as they are played by others.

To appreciate the impact of a social role on its occupant, one must ask about its importance in the person's repertoire of roles. Four dimensions are useful in analyzing the impact of the role on personality development. First, one must ask about the number of roles in which the person is involved. As the number of roles increases, the person's appreciation of the social system as a whole increases. Cognitive complexity, social perspective taking, and interpersonal problem-solving ability would be expected to increase with the number and diversity of social roles (Kohlberg, 1969; Piaget, 1972; Selman, 1971). In fact, Parsons (Parsons & Bales, 1955) has argued that the process of socialization can best be understood as an outcome of participation in a larger number of increasingly diverse and complex social roles. People who resist involvement in new roles could be said to forestall their development by closing off access to new responsibilities as well as new demands.

A second dimension along which roles vary is the intensity of involvement which they demand or which the person brings to the role. Sarbin and Allen (1968) offer an eight-level scale of role involvement, from zero, or noninvolvement, to seven, in which there is no differentiation between the self and the role. At the low end, they give the example of a person whose membership in a club has lapsed for a number of years. Such a position holds no immediate expectations for behavior, although the person could resume greater involvement at any time. At the high end, they give the example of a person who believes he or she is the object of witchcraft. The total being is involved in the role to the extent that death can result from such a belief. Similar examples of very intense role involvement can be offered. In 1979 over 600 people committed mass suicide in the Jonestown massacre in Guyana, South America. All these people closely identified with their religious leader, the Reverend Jim Jones. Jones persuaded his followers to give him all their worldly possessions and to move to Guyana to form a religious community. After some time in Guyana, Jones demanded that these people follow him into death. While a few escaped, Jones and most of the followers drank poison. Shortly afterward, hundreds of people were dead. The total beings of these people were so closely identified with Jones and so intensely involved in their religious roles that they were willing to sacrifice their lives. In a less extreme example, people who choose to become priests or nuns also have a high level of role involvement. They are willing to forsake adult sexual relationships and the chance to have their own families to become totally absorbed in a religious role.

Intense role involvement presumes greater investment of attention and energy, greater emotional commitment to the role, and perhaps greater anxiety about any failure to meet role expectations. The more fused the person becomes with the role, the more likely the personality is to be influenced by socialization pressures that are tied to the role.

A third dimension of the social role is the amount of time the role demands. This dimension is important because a time-consuming role sets up the basic structure for many interactions during each day. Even if a role—let us say the role of gas-station attendant—is not of high intensity, it may involve so many hours per day that the person has few opportunities to enact other roles. In fact, it may be a source of continuing personal frustration if a low-intensity role continues to demand a large number of waking hours.

The fourth dimension of the role that will influence its impact on personality is the degree of structure specified for the role. Social roles differ in the extent to which role expectations are specified and in the degree to which consensus exists about how a role should be performed. Some social roles, such as member of Congress, police officer, or college president, have written criteria for role enactment. These kinds of public figures are generally held accountable to perform the services they were hired, elected, or appointed to provide. The role performer and the audience acknowledge some common list of behaviors as appropriate to the role. Even less-public roles, such as those of secretaries, bookkeepers, and salespeople, have written criteria stating the degree of structure specified for their role. Like public figures, these kinds of workers are expected by employers to perform the services they were hired to do.

Other roles are much less clearly articulated. They may be defined by cultural myths (for example, the role of explorer) or by community norms (for example, the role of neighbor). Enactment of some roles is quite private, viewed only by members of the immediate family or a few close friends. In these instances, one is free to define and to enact the role as it suits those few people who are involved. Lovers, siblings, close friends, and marriage partners can develop relationships along a variety of paths without coming under the scrutiny of elaborate socialization pressures for specific role performances. This does not mean that there are no role expectations for these roles, but simply that there is more room for improvisation.

When roles are highly structured, the issue of person/role fit comes into question. Under conditions of lack of fit, the occupant of the role experiences continual frustration at the demands for performance that are not compatible with his or her temperament, talents, or motives. In contrast, when the fit is comfortable, a highly structured role may provide the reassurance and support that comes from knowing the clear expectations for performance. Under conditions of person/role compatibility, the highly structured role may offer opportunities for the development of new competences that contribute to the maturation and growth of the person. When there is less consensus about a role, occupants generally have greater opportunities to shape the role to reflect personal predispositions. However, loosely defined roles can generate considerable conflict if the people in reciprocal role positions cannot agree about how the roles should be played. So, for example, although the roles of husband and wife have considerable latitude for the expression of personal preferences and values, if the man and woman cannot agree about the expectations for these roles, the marriage will suffer from continual conflict and uncertainty.

The importance of role structure depends as well on the intensity of role involvement. Some highly structured roles stimulate minimal involvement. In fact, the structure makes it possible to perform the role rather automatically, without having to invest a great deal of personal energy in the role. Minimal role structure usually means that the person has to impose some definition about the function of the role and the norms for role enactment. We would expect the level of involvement to be greater when the role is loosely defined, if only because the person has had to give thought and time to the task of defining his or her own conception of the role.

Two additional points help clarify the meaning of the social role. First, each role is usually linked to one or more related roles or reciprocal roles. The student and the teacher, the parent and the child, the salesperson and the customer are in reciprocal roles. Each role is partly defined by the other roles that support it. The function of the role is determined by its relation to the surrounding role groups to which it is allied. Second, each role has associated with it a set of role expectations. Role expectations are held by the person in the role, by those in reciprocal roles, and by the audience who observes the role performance. For example, college students have certain expectations about the role of student. They may expect this role to press them toward logical thought, scholarship, community participation, and camaraderie with new friends. Those in reciprocal roles—professors and instructors—have certain expectations of the college student. They may expect students to attend classes, experience intellectual growth, contribute original, creative ideas to class discussions, and successfully complete class assignments. Finally, the audience who observes the role performance—parents and friends—may expect the college student to get good grades, join a fraternity or sorority, become an independent person, and find a mate. Thus, the role expectations that are expressed for a particular role act as socialization forces, pushing the person toward a more adequate enactment of the role.

Influence of Multiple Roles on Personality

In general, the pattern of increased participation in a greater number of complex roles is viewed as a normal and positive experience. Social-role theorists argue that the underlying mechanism of development is the opportunity to expand one's repertoire of role enactments (Brim, 1966; Nye, 1976; Parsons & Bales, 1955). With the increase in the number of simultaneous roles that a person plays comes a demand to learn new skills of role playing, role differentiation, and role integration. With each new role, the person's self-definition changes, and his or her ability to influence the environment increases (Brim, 1976a). Allport (1955, 1961) argues that the first criterion for a healthy personality is that the person demonstrate an extension of the self. This means that the person derives satisfaction and pleasure from diverse activities, participates in a variety of roles and activities, and shows involvement in meaningful relationships with others. Once again, the example of college student will illustrate the influence of multiple roles on personality. All this suggests that it should be not only normal but growth-producing to participate in many roles simultaneously.

This is not to say that the experience of simultaneously occupying several roles is easy or free from stress. Quite the opposite is true. There is often competition or conflict between the demands of two or more roles. One of the greatest sources of tension during young adulthood is the competition of role demands. Here we think of the tension between demands from the work setting and demands for time to build an intimate relationship with one's spouse or the tension between the desire to have children and the desire for achievement in work (Hoffman, 1974; Hoffman & Nye, 1974). For both men and women, the world of work is likely to provide the greatest test for commitment and the greatest pressures for productivity during the early adulthood years. Particularly in a dual-career family, the desires of the individual partners for occupational success may limit each other's freedom both at work and at home. For example, one report has found that the greater the husband's need for power, the lower the wife's career attainment will be (Winter, Stewart, & McClelland, 1977). Demands from the work setting compete directly with needs for intimacy and with the time and energy available for parenting. Thus, while part of role learning involves a widening of competences and relationships, another part involves balancing the conflicting responsibilities of simultaneous role expectations (Cartwright, 1978; Cortes, 1976; Coser & Rokoff, 1971; Osipow, 1976).

Although the stresses from role conflict can be very great, they may also be a force toward growth. When role demands conflict, the person must begin to set priorities about how much energy can be devoted to each role. In the process of bringing many diverse roles into balance, the person imposes his or her own value system on life's demands. There may be ways to bring diverse roles into harmony or to eliminate roles that are no longer meaningful. In adulthood, the challenges posed by role conflict may foster a reevaluation of personal goals as well as an integration of role behaviors. In striving to resolve role strain, the person can achieve, in each of the roles, competences that can enhance the performance of other roles. Having achieved a workable balance of role commitments, one has the opportunity to function at new levels of effectiveness. We might even hypothesize that the ability to resolve role strain effectively may in itself generate energy that will allow the person to take on additional roles or to perform existing roles with increased vigor. Ineffective efforts to resolve role conflict, however, may detract from role performance in several roles. The failure to resolve role conflict drains energy from the total system. The person who is unable to bring work and family expectations into balance may experience chronic tension, physical symptoms, and disruption in the performance of both the work and family roles. What is more, this cycle of role failure is self-perpetuating. Drained of energy, a person is likely to falter as an effective member of the social system. Inability to be an effective worker may lead to ostracism by other workers, lack of promotion, or being fired. Inability to perform the role of spouse effectively may lead to estrangement, dissolution of the marriage, or social rejection by the extended family or the community. Because many roles are so essential to the maintenance of social organizations, failure at role enactment generally has serious consequences.

Contribution of Social Roles to Personality Change

Entry into new roles across the life span has the potential for stimulating personality development. Three kinds of role change are especially important to the process of reorganization of personality.

Movement through Age Roles

First, there are the successive age roles that are part of every culture's organization (Linton, 1942). In traditional Chinese culture (Ch'ing dynasty, 1644 A.D.–1911 A.D.) development was differentiated into five periods: infancy (birth to age 3 or 4), childhood (4 to 15), adolescence (16 to marriage), fertile adulthood (marriage to about 55), and later adulthood (55 to death) (Levy, 1949). Our own description of psychosocial development (see Chapter 5) includes a ten-stage view of development from conception through later adulthood (Newman & Newman, 1979). The notion of life stages reflects sequential changes in personal competences as well as changes in cultural expectations and demands. At each new stage, the person is able to function more effectively and to master new tasks and begins to focus attention on new areas of concern. At the same time, the culture offers new opportunities, new areas of responsibility, and new areas of restriction. The adolescent in American society, for example, is permitted to drive a car, to buy alcoholic beverages, and to vote—all new opportunities that are not extended to children. The adolescent is also expected to handle more difficult schoolwork, to study independently, to make decisions about a career, and to be fully responsible for any illegal behavior. Personality change at each new life stage can be understood as adaptation to both the opportunities and the restrictions of the new age role. Each age role brings a change in the person's status as well as a change in the range of behaviors that are expected. In order to meet these expectations, the person normally has to acquire new skills. Growth is promoted as the person tries to live up to the expectations for a new age role. The person is also usually expected to give up some of the earlier modes of behavior. The adolescent who threatens to tell his mother about a peer's misbehavior is told to stop acting like a baby. The adult who is very moody, impulsive, and self-centered is described as acting like an adolescent. The older adult who decides to have a hair transplant and a facelift and to try out the singles bars is criticized for refusing to "grow old gracefully." Consensus about the appropriate age for certain life attainments or activities seems to work as a prod to keep people moving along in their socialization as adults (Neugarten, Moore, & Lowe, 1965). Especially in middle and later adulthood, people tend to perceive age-related norms as powerful, motivating guidelines for behavior. Age norms about marriage, parenting, financial independence from parents, emotional independence from parents, and involvement with one's children force many people to give up old, familiar patterns in order to live up to the cultural expectations of a new age role.

Abrupt Entry into New Roles

The second kind of change in roles that prompts personality change is the relatively abrupt entry into new roles. There are some life experiences for which training or preparation is minimal. Some examples are the child's experience as a pupil in the first grade, dating, marriage, parenting, and retirement. Each of these experiences requires new learning on many levels at once. The role requires the development of many new skills, it generally involves increased uncertainty and anxiety, and there is considerable pressure from others in reciprocal roles to achieve effective enactment of the role. Because of the lack of training, one must draw on inner resources to cope with the uncertainty and social pressures tied to these new role positions. Effective coping will lead to the acquisition of new information, new strategies for responding to emerging demands, and the use of existing skills in new, more appropriate ways. What may begin as an anxiety-producing new role can stimulate an important expansion of competence. The satisfactions of the new role eventually bring about greater identification with the functions and norms of that role until the new role becomes integrated into the self-concept. In many instances, the opportunities of a new role bring to the surface latent competences and predispositions of which the person was not aware. The new parent may for the first time identify his or her potential for nurturance or playfulness. The new retiree may discover a latent capacity for intellectual development or for mastery of a manual skill that had never been given the opportunity to flourish.

With each new role, the person changes in two ways. First, the person attempts to meet new demands by making use of existing skills, making the role an extension of what he or she already does well. Second, the person modifies existing skills or acquires new skills in order to function more effectively in the new role. Over time, the person understands the role more fully, plays the role more effectively, and views the role as a less alien part of his or her life pattern.

Attainment of Desired Roles

The third important source of role change is the attainment of desired roles. Whereas age roles are imposed more or less arbitrarily as a function of chronological age, some roles are achieved through effort and skill. Examples of achieved roles to which a person might aspire are: member of a fraternity or sorority, elected leader of a student organization, creator of an important invention, and prominent politician. Beginning in early school age—about age 5 or 6—children develop aspirations about the kind of person they hope to be. These aspirations are sometimes called the "ideal self." They have a moral component in that they provide a standard of excellence to encourage good behavior. Often these early ideals are stated in literal, extreme terms, reflecting the limitations in language and cognition of children of this age. Nonetheless, the ideal self serves an important function, keeping the child bound to an optimistic view of the self as changing and growing in the future. Over time, the ideal self prompts striving toward specific attainments. One may try to make a perfect score on a test, to be the fastest runner on the team, to wear the prettiest dress at school, or to be invited to the most birthday parties. Often, one's ideals are stated in terms of roles. Dutiful daughter, scholar, altar boy, star athlete, and most popular are examples of aspired roles that may reflect the content of the ideal self. People become so involved in attaining desired roles because many motives are being satisfied at the same time. At first, the daughter on the track team may want to be the fastest runner on the team because her parents expect her to be number one in everything she does. The daughter also has a need for approval from her parents. Success on the team satisfies these underlying needs to be valued and cherished at the same time as it satisfies needs for competence, achievement, and peer-group affiliation.

As the person strives to attain these goals, a process of reality-oriented reevaluation takes place. If a desired goal is achieved, the person is encouraged about the attainment of goals and the possibility of success in subsequent effort. One also has an opportunity to evaluate whether these ideals are really satisfying. One might try to become a school leader and then discover that the role is less glamorous or less satisfying than one had expected. There is also a reality-oriented reevaluation that comes from failing to achieve desired roles. When goals are missed, the person begins to redefine personal aspirations so that they more adequately reflect existing competences. Or the person may be highly motivated to strengthen existing competences and try, once again, to attain the goal that is being sought.

Contribution of Social Roles to Stability in Personality

In the preceding section, we have emphasized the potential for change that is brought about through participation in new social roles. Here, we focus on certain long-term roles that bring with them a degree of stability and continuity to each personal history. Four long-term roles are identified that have impact across several life stages: child, parent, male or female, and worker. We do not mean to suggest that these roles are not touched by age-graded expectations. Indeed, they do evolve in response to the changing competences of the person and the changing expectations of the culture. Nevertheless, the persistence of these roles across time and the accumulation of memories, interactions, and conflicts associated with each of these roles give them experiential preeminence in the consolidation of personality.

The Child

The role of the child within a family group is the first role one learns. Initially no other roles compete with it for the person's time and energy. Because it is first, it sets a tone for subsequent role learning. The extent to which expectations for behavior are vague or clear, the tendency to be rewarded for role enactment or punished for failure to enact the role, the sense of reciprocity in role relationships—all these kinds of learning in the role of child create expectations for the pattern of future role learning.

Continuity of the role is supported by stability in the cast of characters. Whereas students have many teachers and many classmates, the roles of mother, father, siblings, aunts, uncles, cousins, and grandparents are usually filled by the same people throughout life. These people tend to retain their view of each person in the family network in terms of his or her generation and ancestry. A first-born will always be first-born in the eyes of the later-born. A grandchild will always be viewed as a grandchild in the eyes of grandparents. Even when the person is no longer a child chronologically, other family members will identify that person as the off-spring of particular parents or the grandchild of particular grandparents.

In addition to being identified as someone's child, one may also be treated as a child long after childhood has ended. The subordinate role of child is likely to be perpetuated in some ways by one's parents well into adulthood. Parents may expect their child to follow their advice, to show respect, or to set aside their own wishes for the parents' wishes. Parents may resist seeing their child as equally competent as or more competent than they. They may refuse to accept their child's advice. They may continue to see themselves as responsible for their child's safety, happiness, or success long after the child desires their help. In one or more ways, the relationship between parent and adult child is bound to retain characteristics that prevailed while the child was young.

The child role contributes to personality in another, more subtle way as well. The parent/child relationship is a model for all types of authority relationships. One first learns how to respond to authority figures by learning how to respond to one's father and mother. According to psychoanalytic theory (Freud, 1917/1963), this parent/child relationship becomes a prototype for later encounters with authorities. One imposes the expectations learned in the child/parent relationship onto other interactions with authorities. Expectations that an authority figure will be critical, arbitrary, supportive, or indifferent are learned as a child from interactions with parents. Because this learning takes place at a young age when the child has little notion of how other families function or about the logic of these interactions, the child is likely to accept these attributes of the parental authority as natural and correct. Even when the person is older and can approach interactions with authority figures from a more autonomous position, the early, emotional learning that was acquired during childhood tints the character of the interactions. For most of us, the child with his or her feelings of vulnerability, shame, and guilt provides a lasting barrier to fully autonomous adult functioning.

The Parent

One of the roles a child observes within the family is the role of parent. During toddlerhood and early-school-age years, children are likely to equate the general concept of mother and father with their own mother and father. We think that all parents act the way our parents act, that all parents believe what ours believe. During the early-school-age period an active process of parental identification occurs. We not only admire our parents, but we become more and more like them. Out of a desire to share their status and power, out of a need for their love and approval, and out of fear of their moments of rage, we take on their mannerisms, we verbalize their opinions, and eventually we internalize their moral standards. Thus, we become parents, in part, during childhood. The aspects of our parents' behaviors, values, and beliefs that are internalized during childhood contribute to the formation of enduring personality characteristics. Some children whose parents were aggressive continue to use and to approve of aggressive strategies in interpersonal interactions in adulthood (Chwast, 1972). Children of parents who encourage autonomy and who give their children responsibility in decision making continue to demonstrate independence in their own behavior and to adhere to a mature, cognitively complex moral code (Baumrind, 1971).

The role of parent, when it is actually enacted by caring for one's own children, lasts as long as one's children are alive. A variety of expectations are associated with the parent role. They include providing for the safety and health of the child, providing emotional support and warmth, communicating cultural norms and values, and inducing appropriate behavior through some system of rewards and punishments. Parents generally feel most uncomfortable about their function as socialization agents (Gecas, 1976). Decisions about punishment, limit setting, or offering rewards and incentives frequently stimulate conflict between the parents. What is more, parents stand between their children and their own parents, often having to justify their socialization strategy to the older generation.

The parent role and all its functions call forth areas of competence that may not be well developed. Parents must be able to anticipate the needs of their children, using nonverbal cues as well as verbal signals to identify those needs. Parents must be able to respond to the changing competences of their children, offering stimulation and resources that are appropriate to the child's developmental level. As the socialization process continues, children will question the decisions, rules, and punishments their parents impose. Parents must be able to articulate the rationale behind those restrictions or decisions, helping children identify the logic of the socialization mechanisms. The need to clarify values for one's children leads to the need to clarify them for oneself. The parent role stimulates an active assessment of one's values and an ongoing commitment to those values in the decisions one makes for or about one's children.

The opportunities to do things for one's children, to offer nurturance and warmth, to defend or protect one's children, to educate them, to impose restrictions, to punish and to reward, and to anticipate their future needs provide avenues for personal expression that may not be found in other roles. The parent role can be a means of enacting a range of personal values with the goal of creating a meaningful life experience for one's children. Because the role expectations for parental behavior are not clearly stipulated, the parent role can be an avenue for the elaborate expression of personality. One's own talents, temperament, and motives can be blended in their own unique way in order to establish an intimate, life-long bond between parent and child.

Sex Role

In addition to age-graded expectations, cultures have expectations for the behavior of males and females. An important component of the socialization process is to teach children the skills, mannerisms, and values they will need to function as men or as women in the culture. Sensitivity to gender differences begins in toddlerhood as 2-year-olds learn to apply gender labels, such as *girl* and *boy, mommy* and *daddy,* or *man* and *woman.* By nursery school age—that is, 3 or 4—children already show evidence of having learned certain sex-role expectations. Preschool children show a preference for same-sex playmates (Thompson, 1975). They designate certain toys as girls' or boys' toys and resist playing with the toys designated as inappropriate to their sex (Flerx, Fidler, & Rogers, 1976). Sex-role standards that are learned early in childhood tend to have an absolute quality that reflects the child's conceptual level. Differences between boys and girls are thought of as absolute rather than as points along a continuum. Girls wear sandals, boys do not. Boys wrestle, girls do not. Whatever the culture prescribes as essentially masculine or feminine behavior, these prescriptions are learned at an early age, before any logical evaluation of them can take place.

Sex-role standards influence not only the range of behavior that is viewed as appropriate at the moment but the aspirations or goals one sets for the future. During elementary school, boys fantasy about a wide range of future occupations, including policeman, doctor, astronaut, and athlete. Girls, in contrast, fantasy about a very limited range of careers—fashion model, teacher, nurse.

In a retrospective study of career plans among college women, Harmon (1971) asked students to respond to a list of 135 occupations. For each occupation, the subject was asked whether she had ever considered it as a career, the age at which she had first thought of it, and the age at which she had rejected it. The pattern of responses showed that the most popular and earliest occupational choices were housewife and actress. These were first considered in the age range 6–9, and thereafter many of the subjects continued to look forward to becoming housewives. Later choices tended to be more specific and reflected more understanding of actual professions. For example, careers such as nurse and veterinarian were chosen at age 10 or 12, whereas biologist, nurse's aide, and physical therapist were chosen at around 15. The subjects also tended to express interest in a narrow range of career choices. Fewer than 3% of the sample had ever thought of such careers as accountant, governor, dentist, weather forecaster, museum director, children's clothes designer, or hotel manager, to name just a few.

As boys and girls look around at what it means to be an adult in their culture, they identify the roles that men and women play. The visibility of males in certain occupations and females in others reinforces the formulation of sex-typed career aspirations. We would argue, then, that early sex-role learning carries with it prescriptions for future as well as contemporary behavior that influences important life choices.

The sex-role script does not remain unaltered. During later adolescence, there is a reevaluation of one's sex-role identity that incorporates important changes that have occurred since childhood. First, sexual maturation brings about changes in body image and changes in sexual impulses that demand inclusion in the sex-role definition. Second, experiences with dating and the norms for determining popularity influence one's perception of oneself as a socially desirable (or undesirable) male or female. Finally, cognitive maturation permits reflection on the validity of existing sex-role expectations. As part of their work on identity formation, adolescents begin to consider how to express their maleness or femaleness in a way that is congruent with other dimensions of their personality. That may mean rejecting some of the existing sex-role norms in favor of expressing certain components of temperament, talent, or motivation. As we saw in the study by Block discussed in Chapter 2, males are more likely to build on patterns of personal characteristics that are established during the early adolescent period. Marked change after that time is associated with stress and instability. Females who take less traditional views of sex-role behavior are more likely to have opportunities for continued personality change.

Part of the adolescent reformulation of the sex role will include some judgments about the desire to marry, to have children, or to pursue a particular career. The less committed women are to a traditional definition of the female sex role, including marriage and childbearing, the more likely they are to choose a career that is not commonly entered by women (Tittle, Chitayat, & Denker, 1977). We see, then, that the nature of the sex-role identity that is achieved in later adolescence has important implications for subsequent life choices. Some argue that those males and females who are least bound to a narrow definition of sex-appropriate behaviors are able to make use of a greater range of behaviors in their own interactions. Adoption of a nontraditional, or "transcendent" (Rebecca, Hefner, & Oleshansky, 1976), sex role permits the flexible use of the full array of interpersonal and cognitive modes for coping with life's challenges.

The Worker Role

Long before the establishment of a professional identity or commitment to a particular occupation, progress is made on the concept of self as worker. Havighurst (1964) has identified three stages in the emergence of the psychological concept of being a worker. In the first stage, children identify with workers, especially parents, relatives, and older siblings. During this process, children come to idealize some work roles. Working becomes an essential component of the ideal self. In the second phase, children acquire a sense of industry. The strategies of being an effective worker, including planning a task, organizing one's time, enjoying feelings of accomplishment, and beginning to evaluate one's progress, are all being learned. The third phase is acquiring an identity as a worker in an occupational role. This may include technical training, on-the-job experience, or experimentation with a variety of work roles. The concept of becoming a worker provides a focus for fantasies, aspirations, and skill development all through childhood and adolescence.

Imposed on these changing conceptualizations of the self as worker are the actual experiences of working. In childhood, families may expect children to perform designated chores or to contribute their effort to community tasks. In adolescence, young people may be hired by others to perform services. In some communities, adolescents are the primary labor force for a variety of settings, including restaurants, grocery stores, and gas stations (Barker & Schoggen, 1973). Young people may also encounter the frustrations of looking for work, of being fired, or of remaining unemployed. These early work experiences help to clarify the direction of career aspirations as well as to socialize young people toward acceptable enactment of the worker role. By the end of later adolescence, most people have found a match between their own skills and interests and some occupation. As part of identity, career commitment reflects an integration of personal values, competences, and future aspirations.

In early and middle adulthood, the worker role generally takes people through a phase of work search and then selection of a relatively stable career (Brim, 1968). In the work search, the worker learns about the characteristics of various jobs. These characteristics include the technical skills required, the authority relations of the organization, the unique norms for role performance, and the expectations for interpersonal relations. In response to these characteristics, the new worker must evaluate the compatibility of his or her own personality with work demands. Each new job helps the person clarify personal competences and temperamental characteristics as they interact with the expectations for role enactment. The final commitment to a career, often in middle adulthood, is built on a process of successive approximations to a satisfying career brought about by rejection from the work setting or rejection by the individual.

In middle adulthood, the worker role generally brings people to their peak in leadership, competence, earning power, and creative contribution. Once the apprenticeship of early adulthood is over, the worker role can offer an avenue for creative contribution to the organization, to the consumer, or to the larger community.

The establishment of a career requires a good fit between individual characteristics and job demands. Once this fit is clarified, the worker role can enhance many of the person's attributes. Opportunities for satisfying needs for achievement, for competence, for social approach, or for power are all potential elements of the work setting. Of course, the work setting may also frustrate these and other motives. Part of the challenge of the worker role is the mutual gratification of personal and occupational needs. When this mutual gratification occurs, the person experiences the satisfaction of knowing that the same behaviors that contribute to a sense of personal competence and industry also contribute to the growth of the work setting. In this way, there is a gradual fusion of the self and the worker role.

Conclusions

We have considered four long-term roles that contribute to stability in personality over the life span. Several mechanisms in the process of role learning and role enactment would appear to account for the unifying impact of these roles. First, at an early age, norms for each of these roles are internalized. That means that long before some of the roles will be enacted, we have expectations about appropriate role performance. Through identification and modeling, young children become committed to a version of themselves as parents, males or females, and workers.

Second, a consequence of early role identification is the formation of aspirations about future role enactment. These aspirations direct life choices, and consequently the opportunities for the expression of personal talents, temperament, or motives are channeled toward the achievement of role-related aspirations.

Third, each of these roles has relatively open-ended criteria for enactment in our society. That means that in adulthood each role provides an opportunity to enhance certain competences or to emphasize personal characteristics through one's definition of the role. The kind of parent a person becomes, the kind of man or woman, the kind of worker, the kind of adult child are all expressions of the dominant needs and strengths the person brings to the role. Of course, if the criteria for role performance are narrowly defined, then the risk of role conflict can provide a serious challenge to adaptation. When other people in reciprocal role groups hold views about the role that are seriously discrepant from one's own, the resilience of one's personality is put to the test. One may modify or inhibit aspects of personality in order to fit the role, or one may reject the role, thereby closing off a major link between oneself and the larger social community.

Finally, in middle and later adulthood, we are involved in the task of teaching these lifelong roles to others. Here we have the opportunity to evaluate those aspects of the role that were productive and those that were ineffective. We can share some of our unique interpretations of the roles with those who follow. As we participate in the socialization of the next generation, be it as parents, as teachers, as workers, or as community resources, we have an opportunity to pass on our own unique conceptualizations of these vital roles and give them continuity into the future.

Cultural Variations in Roles and Role Expectations

In the two previous sections, we have illustrated some of the ways that participation in social roles contributes to change and stability of personality. The theme that has been raised repeatedly is the importance of considering the degree of fit between the person's competences, temperament, and motives and the demands of the social roles for certain kinds of behavior. In this final section, we add another dimension of variability to this picture. Very simply, every society has its own array of roles and, more important, its own pattern of role expectations. A role may have the same label in two cultures, but expectations for role enactment may be vastly different. The following examples of cultural differences in the role of child, father, and wife suggest just a fraction of the cultural variability that is built into social roles.

There are many ways that children can be integrated into the family group. One dimension of the child role that differs from culture to culture is the extent to which children assist in the family's economic survival and household maintenance. Children may be treated as helpless, as demanding resources but providing none, or as providing important economic contributions to the family. Three examples of children's participation in family economics follow.

Hottentot, South Africa (Schapera, 1930)

"From the moment it can stand on its feet the child, although still dependent upon its mother, gradually learns to fend for itself in its environment. Hottentot children grow rather slowly, probably, says Schultze, because of the scanty nourishment. In poorer families they are shown by the mother how to dig out roots and bulbs for themselves; they learn to catch mice, lizards, and similar small animals, which they roast on the fire; seek out wild honey, and so on. In the more wealthy families each child is allotted a special cow for his own use, which he may milk for himself in the morning and evening" (p. 134).*

---

* From *The Kliorsan Peoples of South Africa*, by I. Schapera. Copyright 1930 by Routledge & Kegan Paul Ltd., London. This and all other quotations from this source are reprinted by permission.

Frang, Cameroon (Trézenem, 1936)	"As soon as the child is old enough to eat like adults, and talks and counts properly, he starts accompanying his parents to the fields and to fishing; he learns to swim, paddle, dance, and play the tomtom and various musical instruments. The little girls learn to cultivate a small piece of farm land which is given them by their mothers" (p. 71).
Ukraine (Koenig, 1939)	"Children mean additional working hands, and hence an increased source of income to the peasant's household. When scarcely eight years of age he runs all sorts of errands, carries his father's lunch out to the distant fields all by himself, rides the horses to water, drives the cattle out to the pasture—in a word, learns to depend on himself. At the age of twelve he already performs practically all the tasks of an adult . . . sometimes working even harder than his parents" (p. 284).

From these examples, we begin to see that the way the child role is defined will interact with important dimensions of personality. If the child has valued talents, these talents will be enhanced and the child's sense of worth will increase. If the child cannot perform expected role behaviors, the child may incorporate feelings of shame and worthlessness. At a more general level, expectations that the child will be able to make important contributions to the family group may generate a commitment to the role of worker and a sense of the interdependence in which all members of the family recognize their reliance on the contributions of others.

The role of father is also interpreted differently across cultures. Observations of father/infant interactions at home during the first months of life find that American fathers do not speak to their babies frequently, and few take any regular responsibility for the care of their infants (Ban & Lewis, 1974; Kotelchuck, 1972; Lewis & Weinraub, 1976; Rebelsky & Hanks, 1971). In general, American middle-class fathers spend more of their time with infants in play than in caregiving (Kotelchuck, 1976; Lamb, 1975).

The relative separation of American fathers and their newborns can be compared with patterns of father/infant interactions in other cultures. West and Konner (1976) have compared the father/infant relationship in five subsistence cultures. At one extreme of noninvolvement are the Thonga of South Africa (Junod, 1927), who "do not relate to infants or young children except in occasional ritual events" (p. 196). A variety of taboos prevent fathers from having contact with infants under 3 months old. At the other end of the continuum are the !Kung San (Bushmen) of Botswana (West & Konner, 1976). !Kung fathers work about half the days of the week. "They often hold and fondle even the youngest infants, though they return them to the mother whenever they cry and for all forms of routine care. Young children frequently go to them, touch them, talk to them and request food from them and such approaches are almost never rebuffed" (p. 193). Yet !Kung fathers were rarely present during observations made with infants under 26 weeks of age. However, with children 2 to 6 years of age, fathers were present during 30% of observations.

If we want to think of implications, the cultural definition of the father role will determine the extent to which it is an outlet for the expression of nurturance and warmth. Boys will be prepared early in childhood to develop the skills necessary for role enactment. If the father is viewed mainly as "the breadwinner," his socialization will differ considerably from that of the father who is viewed as caregiver and protector. What is more, the child's aspirations about fulfilling the role will depend on the status attributed to the role by the culture.

The role of wife, like that of father, has implications for personality development during childhood as one observes husbands and wives interacting, in adolescence as one fantasizes about marriage, and in adulthood as one enacts the wife role. An important component of the wife role is the degree of status accorded her by her husband, her extended family, her children, and her community. In a number of societies, husbands are clearly dominant over their wives (Stephens, 1963). This dominance may be expressed in wife beating, overt signs of deference, such as bowing to or walking behind the male, or customs relating to ownership and decision making. The following excerpt (from a description of marriage in Buganda) illustrates a male-dominant orientation:

> The wife is expected to take a subordinate position; she should obey her husband and he is entitled to beat her if she does not do so. The household is organized for his convenience; meals should be ready at the times when he likes to eat, and the wife should not cook for herself in his absence. She should ask his permission to go visiting, and if she goes away from home to sleep he fixes the number of days that she may be away [Mair, 1940, p. 13].

In other societies, men and women each have responsibilities, possessions, and rights that give them comparable power. The following excerpt suggests a culture in which women have a role that is respected and admired.

> The status of the wife in Hottentot society is far from being that of an inferior. Although as a rule she plays a subordinate role in matters pertaining to tribal life, and in public always walks several paces behind her husband, yet her position in the household is supreme, and the education of the children is wholly in her hands. She is regarded as the mistress of the hut, which she brings with her at marriage, and of all its contents.

She even has the right in certain circumstances to forbid her husband to enter it. She has her own property in cattle, some given to her by her parents while she was still a child, others when she was married, and her husband will not venture to sell or slaughter an animal belonging to her without her consent or in her absence. Even if he intends to barter his own stock he usually first consults her, and during his absence she also controls the pasturing of the herds. She supervises or herself does the milking which provides the household with most of its food, and controls all the provisions, allotting to each his food according to status and age, and brooking no contradiction. Her husband may not even take a mouthful of milk without first obtaining her permission, and should he do so, says Hahn, his nearest female relatives will put a fine on him [Schapera, 1930, p. 251].

The analysis of power in a family is not a simple one. In some societies, the spouse who controls the most resources, including money, property, education, or material goods, will have the most power. However, in other societies, the more highly educated men who also have access to an abundance of resources tend to share their power more fully with their wives. Thus, control of resources is not the sole predictor of family power. One must also ask about the cultural norm for egalitarianism (Rodman, 1972).

Once again, the cultural definition of the wife role will influence the kinds of competences that are encouraged, the socialization toward independence or dependence, and the internalization of values about how wives ought to be treated. The woman in one society who might be viewed as an undesirable wife because she is too "headstrong" or too interested in financial matters would be viewed as a desirable wife in another culture for just these same qualities.

In short, as we learn the cultural definition of important life roles, we also learn to value or devalue certain aspects of our own personality. We begin to perceive ourselves as ill suited or well suited to enact these roles. We also internalize a set of aspirations about these roles that contribute to the ideal self and direct major life choices.

Chapter Five

Crisis and Coping

Every life story is accented by periods of unusual stress that we call crises. During these periods the normal flow of daily activities and interactions is disrupted. One needs new resources, new skills, or a new conceptualization to meet the challenges of these times of crisis. At these periods, the personality is most readily understood through observation of the coping strategies the person uses. Coping is a primary mechanism in the process of adaptation. Coping includes the wide array of efforts that a person makes to anticipate and to resolve stress in order to create new life solutions to the challenges presented by the crisis. The goal of the coping behavior is to maintain the person's basic personality and to allow the person to use the strengths of this personality to meet the challenge effectively. This not only gives people new solutions and a new repertoire of skills and abilities, but it also gives them new confidence in themselves.

When adolescents go to college, many are away from home for the longest period in their lives so far. Some experience a crisis of separation. This is a crisis both students and parents have expected and probably even planned for. This planning would be a natural coping effort in anticipation of the crisis in order to help both parents and students deal with the stresses imposed by the separation. A wide range of emotions may be aroused at the separation. All these conditions will lead to a heightened state of stress. Without going into the details of a particular coping effort, let us say that most students will learn of the value of their own personality in a situation in which they are primarily alone. They will use this resource in developing an adjustment to college life, an adjustment which is uniquely their own, which may be stressful, and which may lead them to become more effective people. New skills, new resources, and new conceptualizations are used to meet the challenge of this crisis. The students will have learned many things and will gain lasting confidence in their own ability to manage. The next time a separation crisis arises, they will be able to cope with it more effectively. Finally, as they gain an increased awareness of their personality resources, they can add this to their theory of themselves.

In this chapter, the concepts of crisis and coping will be discussed in detail. The goal is to begin to appreciate the implications of person/environment interactions during periods of crisis for the crystallization of personality.

Life Crises

We can think of life crises along three dimensions. First, some crises are linked to a developmental time frame and are therefore somewhat predictable. Entering first grade at age 6, having a first child in the twenties or early thirties, and losing one's spouse in the late sixties or early seventies are examples of crises that are likely enough that they deserve anticipatory thought. Other crises, such as a flood, early death of a parent, or death of a child, are less likely and highly unpredictable. Crisis can also be chronic or temporary. Some families repeatedly experience unemployment, whereas for other families job loss is a sudden and shocking occurrence that is quickly followed by a new job search and continued employment. Finally, crisis can be the consequence of personal incompetence, or it can be the consequence of fate, environmental disaster, or deliberate manipulation by others. Of course this last dimension depends heavily on the person's point of view. One woman might blame herself for the dissolution of her marriage, feeling that she had not been attractive or clever or devoted enough to keep her husband. Another woman might blame the husband, the secretary, the community, or the weather for her husband's lack of affection. In fact, the perception of any set of events as a crisis depends heavily on the perceiver. Feelings of helplessness, vulnerability, or guilt may contribute to the interpretation of the self as responsible for the crisis. In contrast, feelings of high self-esteem, efficacy, and pride all contribute to a belief that crisis is not of one's own making and certainly not insurmountable. Two rather different approaches to the analysis of life crises provide a contrast that helps us appreciate the importance of this concept for the study of personality. Normative life crises are periodic, predictable stress points that are built into the life course. Unpredictable life stresses, or dialectical asynchronies, are crisis periods that may or may not be encountered. Some lives are more heavily dotted with such crisis events than others, producing greater demand on the coping system.

Normative Life Crises

In *Development through Life: A Psychosocial Approach* (1979), we have presented a developmental analysis of psychosocial development. This approach is an integration of the work of Erik Erikson's concept of psychosocial crisis and Robert Havighurst's concept of developmental tasks. In that book, we have used the research literature in order to posit a list of tasks that people work on at different points during their lives. We have expanded Erikson's crises from eight to nine so that they will correspond with the life organization in American culture, and we have theorized about the central process through which the psychosocial crisis is normally and successfully resolved. Many of the concepts in the following discussion flow from the contributions of Erik Erikson (1950, 1959). If the reader is interested in finding out more about the concepts of psychosocial theory, we would suggest pursuing some of the works mentioned above.

In psychosocial theory, the concept of crisis refers to the person's psychological efforts to adjust to the demands of the social environment at nine chronological stages of development (Newman & Newman, 1979; see Table 5–1). The word *crisis* in this context refers to a normal set of

Table 5-1. Psychosocial Crises of Nine Life Stages

Life Stage	Psychosocial Crisis
Infancy (birth to 2 years)	Trust versus mistrust
Toddlerhood (2–4)	Autonomy versus shame and doubt
Early school age (5–7)	Initiative versus guilt
Middle school age (8–12)	Industry versus inferiority
Early adolescence (13–17)	Group identity versus alienation
Later adolescence (18–22)	Individual identity versus role diffusion
Young adulthood (23–30)	Intimacy versus isolation
Middle adulthood (31–50)	Generativity versus stagnation
Later adulthood (51–)	Integrity versus despair

stresses and strains rather than an extraordinary set of events. The theory postulates that at each stage of development the society in which a person lives makes certain psychic demands on him or her. These demands differ from stage to stage. The demands are experienced by the person as mild but persistent guidelines and expectations for behavior. As people near the end of a particular stage of development, they are forced to make some type of resolution, adjusting themselves to the demands of society while simultaneously translating the societal demands into personal terms.

This process produces a state of tension within the person that must be reduced in order for the person to proceed to the next stage. It is this tension state that is called the psychosocial crisis. The psychosocial crisis of a stage forces the person to use developmental skills that have only recently been mastered. There is, therefore, an interrelation between the developmental tasks of each stage and the psychosocial crisis of that stage. In addition, resolutions of previous crises influence resolutions of current and future crises. The person uses all personal talents and skills learned in previous stages to adjust to a current crisis. These are never enough in themselves, and the person is forced to develop new social skills in successfully resolving the crisis.

Table 5–1 lists the crisis of each of the stages of development, from infancy through later adulthood. The crises are expressed in polarities—trust versus mistrust, autonomy versus shame and doubt—suggesting the nature of a successful or unsuccessful resolution of the crisis at each stage. A completely unsuccessful resolution is quite unlikely. Each person, however, is expected to experience some element of the negative pole in an effort to confront and resolve the crisis of each stage.

The concept of normative life crises has important implications for the study of personality development. First, it emphasizes the principle that growth involves psychological tension. As one makes the transition from stage to stage, one undergoes periods of increased uncertainty about one's capacity to meet coming demands and, perhaps, some resistance to leaving the stability of an earlier stage. This combination of uncertainty and resistance generates anxiety. We often tend to interpret anxiety as a negative sign, a sign of danger or threat. One implication of the notion of normative crisis is that anxiety can serve as a signal and even as a motivational force for work that is necessary in order for growth to continue. In fact, the idea of normative crisis would suggest that developmental anxiety—that is, anxiety about one's ability to succeed at developmental tasks of each life stage—may be a continuous part of life, waxing and waning during one's movement through each developmental stage. If one can learn to recognize this anxiety as a signal of growth, movement, and transition, one can begin to focus attention on those aspects of life experience that appear to be changing.

A second implication of the notion of normative crisis is, of course, that the resolution of each life stage involves some balance between the positive and negative poles of the crisis. Just like the moon, every person has a "dark" side, an array of life experiences, feelings, and wishes that are perceived by the self as unacceptable. We all have a negative identity, a part of ourselves that we devalue, that we may even deny as representing anything significant in our personality. People who are functioning well and who feel a great sense of personal fulfillment in their daily lives still encounter moments of discouragement. They may see a discrepancy between the intimacy they desire and the feeling of separateness they actually experience, or they may have a sense of futility in the face of efforts to make a meaningful contribution to their social group. Rather than trying to deny or ignore these experiences, we must begin to understand their contribution to personal growth. To what extent is the feeling of isolation a necessary outcome of a well-defined personal identity? To what extent does stagnation represent resistance to the threat of mortality? How might feelings of despair reflect a person's inability to accept the end of change and growth after a lifetime of seeking to grow? These thoughts suggest a need for further research on the crises of adulthood and a new conceptual orientation toward the role of the negative poles of the life crises in the healthy development of the person.

A third point to be made about normative crises is that positive resolutions of earlier crises may make later crises easier to resolve. At each stage, the challenges of development are very great. Because of the characteristics of one's spouse or the personalities of one's children or the particular stresses and demands of the work setting, adults may discover that they are unable to make a fulfilling adaptation during middle adulthood even though they have successfully resolved earlier crises. In fact, it appears that the adult crises tend to pit the integrity of the individual's personal development against the social, economic and political fluctuations of the historical period. In contemporary society, we see men who were socialized to be independent and competitive being asked to assume greater involvement in the nurturance and care of young children. We see women who have strong needs for affection and approval compelled to participate in bureaucracies in the world of work. The role of parent is bombarded on one side by the demands of the employer and on the other by the lure of self-indulgence and "swinging." Competence and productivity in the worker role are often severely limited by the complexity of the work setting, counterproductive work norms, and the frustration that one's income can never catch up with the rising cost of living. It is a great challenge to be able to provide those adults who are experiencing tension in their efforts to resolve the crises of intimacy, generativity, and integrity with both the historical perspective and the personal skills that will permit them to evolve a personally fulfilling life pattern.

Unpredictable Life Stresses

Because normative life crises are tied to the cultural age-graded expectations for new levels of functioning at each stage of life, we can anticipate them and perhaps even prepare ourselves so as to make the most of each developmental shift. In contrast, there are an array of life stresses that are not readily predictable and do not necessarily occur in a developmental sequence. Some of these stresses may be predictable for large populations, such as the rate of infant mortality or the rate of divorce, but individuals generally cannot predict whether their own child is going to die or whether their own marriage will end in divorce.

To study the impact of stress, it is necessary to have some yardstick to measure the intensity of life events. Meyer (1948) argued that both positive and negative life events could produce stress. He found that there were temporal links between major life events and physical and mental disorders. Building on this idea, Holmes and Rahe (1967) developed the Social Readjustment Rating Scale to measure the perceived stressfulness of 43 life events. Subjects were given the list of events and told that the event of marriage had a value of 50 Life Change Units. They were then asked to score all the other events on a scale from 0 to 100, using the value of 50 for marriage as a point of reference. Table 5–2 shows the average ratings by over 5,000 subjects in Europe, the United States, Central America, Oceania, and Japan. Interestingly, only six life events were viewed as requiring greater adjustment than marriage. This suggests that marriage may not have been a true midpoint in the list of life events. Stated another way, marriage may be one of the more stressful events encountered in many people's lives.

An important observation in the assessment of stress is that both positive and negative events can create stress. In part, the degree of stress may be related to the way the event is perceived (Lazarus, 1974). One person may perceive a life change to be threatening while another person perceives the same change as exhilarating. (Young adults going away to college offer a good illustration of how the same life changes may be perceived differently. Two young men from a small, rural community are going to the same college at the end of the summer. It is the first time either has been away from his family and friends. One of the young men is quite worried that the college, which is located in a big city, will be an unfriendly, lonely, and threatening place. The other is excited about the many new people and experiences such a college and city offer.) However, any life change that requires a reorganization of life activities or a reconceptualization of selfhood will absorb a great amount of energy and personal resources. From this point of view, joyous events have the same stress potential as tragic events.

Every stress event requires adaptation. The extent to which the event is disruptive may depend on the kind of preparation the person has made in anticipation of the event. Stress events also tend to be more difficult when several occur simultaneously. For example, Riegel (1975) describes the possibility of crisis emerging from the asynchrony of life events. Crisis occurs when there are strong, competing claims for limited resources or when heightened uncertainty in one role leads to deficient performance in other roles. For example, starting a new job and having a baby at the same time may be viewed as a crisis of asynchrony. The simultaneous occurrence of retirement and widowhood would be a potential source of crisis. Although many of life's events appear to move in harmony with new skills building neatly on earlier achievements, a normal life can also be seen as replete with discord and contradiction. One may be hired for a job for which one is not qualified. One may marry a person who does not share one's personal aspirations. One may live in a commu-

Table 5–2. Social Readjustment Rating Scale

Rank	Life Event	Stress Value, in Life Change Units
1.	Death of spouse	100
2.	Divorce	73
3.	Marital separation	65
4.	Jail term	63
5.	Death of close family member	63
6.	Personal injury or illness	53
7.	Marriage	50
8.	Fired from job	47
9.	Marital reconciliation	45
10.	Retirement	45
11.	Change in health of family member	44
12.	Pregnancy	40
13.	Sex difficulties	39
14.	Gain of new family member	39
15.	Business readjustment	39
16.	Change in financial state	38
17.	Death of close friend	37
18.	Change to different line of work	36
19.	Change in number of arguments with spouse	35
20.	Mortgage over $10,000	31
21.	Foreclosure of mortgage or loan	30
22.	Change in responsibilities at work	29
23.	Son or daughter leaving home	29
24.	Trouble with in-laws	29
25.	Outstanding personal achievement	28
26.	Wife begins or stops work	26
27.	Begin or end school	26
28.	Change in living conditions	25
29.	Revision of personal habits	24
30.	Trouble with boss	23
31.	Change in work hours or conditions	20
32.	Change in residence	20
33.	Change in schools	20
34.	Change in recreation	19
35.	Change in church activities	19
36.	Change in social activities	18
37.	Mortgage or loan less than $10,000	17
38.	Change in sleeping habits	16
39.	Change in number of family get-togethers	15
40.	Change in eating habits	15
41.	Vacation	13
42.	Christmas	12
43.	Minor violations of the law	11

Adapted from "The Social Readjustment Rating Scale," by T. H. Holmes and R. H. Rahe, *Journal of Psychosomatic Research*, 1967, *11*, 213–218. Copyright 1967, Pergamon Press, Ltd. Reprinted by permission of the authors and publisher.

nity where one is a victim of racial or ethnic prejudice. Examples of potential life conflicts are numerous. The important point is that people are not necessarily devastated by these conflicts. In fact, some seek out conflict as a more desirable alternative to the boredom of predictability. The existence of asynchrony in people's lives promotes a need for new resources, skills, and aspirations that is likely to stimulate personal growth.

Coping Styles

Coping refers to a person's active efforts to resolve stress and to create new solutions to the challenges of each developmental stage (Erikson, 1959). The idea emphasizes the personal resources and competences that are brought to bear on each new environmental challenge. Coping is often contrasted with defense as a mechanism for responding to stress (Kroeber, 1963). Defense generally has as its goal protecting the integrity of the ego. It is an instinctive response to internal and/or external threats (A. Freud, 1936). Usually, the protection requires some distortion of reality. The extent of the distortion varies. For example, in rationalization there is minimal distortion. In the process of rationalization, the real reason for doing something is replaced with an acceptable reason (McKeachie, Doyle, & Moffet, 1976). The unacceptable wishes or events are recognized and explained away through a series of arguments or explanations that appear logical to the person but may be highly subjective to an outside observer. In contrast, a defense such as repression is a global distortion of reality. In the process of repression, the stressful event or thought is simply removed from conscious awareness. All normal people use both coping strategies and defense mechanisms in their efforts to maintain control over their emotions in stressful situations.

Coping emphasizes mastery of the situation rather than protection of the self. This is not to imply that there is no concern for self-protection. In fact, the coping process affirms the commitment to a strong, competent, effective self that insists on confronting each life challenge. White (1974) offers three components of the coping process that emphasize the orientation toward growth. First, coping requires the ability to gain and process new information. New information is required if the person is to redefine the situation or establish some new position in the face of threat. Second, coping requires the ability to maintain control over one's emotional state. This does not mean that one eliminates emotional responses. Rather, it suggests the importance of a capacity to correctly interpret emotions, to express them when necessary, and to limit their expression when necessary. Third, coping requires the ability to move freely in one's environment. This third criterion suggests that at times flight may be a legitimate coping strategy.

Coping Strategies

People use different strategies for coping with stress. At this point there is no comprehensive, widely accepted model for categorizing consistent personality differences in coping styles. Rather, there are separate observations of responses to specific kinds of stress. These observations alert us to the contribution of personality to the coping process. One of the repeated themes in these studies of coping is the role of denial in response to stress. People differ in how seriously they treat the stress, how fully they are willing to accept the severity of the situation, or how vulnerable they will allow themselves to be to environmental conflict.

Janis (1962) observed that people responded in two quite different ways to a "near miss," or close brush with danger. Some felt a heightened anxiety about their own mortality. They had never realized how vulnerable they were. Others saw the same situation as evidence for their resilience. Having come so close to death, they interpreted their survival as evidence that they were meant to continue living. A similar distinction has been observed among combat pilots, civilians who survived an air raid, and survivors of a tornado. The narrow escape made some people increasingly anxious about the threat of potential disasters, while others were confirmed in their belief of invulnerability (Janis, 1974).

Wolff, Friedman, Hofer, and Mason (1964) observed the bereavement process in parents whose children were dying of leukemia. Some parents relied heavily on denial to minimize the stress. They felt sure that their child would not die and that some cure would be found. Other parents, who did not deny the seriousness of their child's illness, showed far greater emotional and physical signs of stress. They were not able to use denial to buffer the pain of the crisis. During the prolonged illness, the parents who could deny the seriousness of their child's condition were able to protect themselves from the stress and continued to have a hopeful, optimistic outlook. The study does not tell us what happened after the children died. One might expect that parents who had denied the seriousness and hopelessness of the illness would be much more devastated by the child's death than those who had begun to grieve while the child was still alive.

The capacity to buffer oneself against the emotional intensity of a situation can protect some people from the stresses that generate illness, anxiety, and fatigue. In an experimental test of this concept, subjects were shown films of woodshop accidents in which serious injuries were depicted. They saw two films without any viewing instructions. Then, half the subjects were instructed to detach themselves from the third film and then to try to totally involve themselves in the fourth film. The other subjects were given the opposite instructions, involvement preceding detachment.

Despite the pain and serious consequences of the accidents, subjects were able to control their feelings. Measures of heart rate and subjective reports of emotional experiences indicated that cognitive strategies, such as reminding oneself that the film participants were actors, were effective in minimizing the impact of stress (Koriat, Melkman, Averill, & Lazarus, 1972). As discussed above, in real situations, without the benefit of coaching or instructions, people seem to differ in their natural capacity to resist stress. Whether the crisis is the stress of the work setting, separation, or death, the ability to minimize its impact is associated with better physical health and greater self-acceptance (Tanner, 1976).

So you will not think that coping always involves minimizing the impact of environmental events, consider quite the opposite coping strategy, which Janis, Mahl, Kagan, and Holt (1969) have described as "the work of worrying," or "emotional inoculation." This concept was based primarily on observations of patients who were undergoing major surgery. In one study, three groups of patients were identified. The first group showed intense preoperative fear and continued anxiety after surgery. Their feelings of vulnerability produced a constant state of emotionality and fear. The second group had little anticipatory anxiety. They were cheerful and calm before surgery, but afterward they were angry, bitter about their treatment, and feeling highly vulnerable. The third group was described as showing moderate anticipatory fear. They were concerned about particular aspects of the operation and tried to find out as much as they could about it. They were somewhat anxious before surgery but tried to remain calm by distracting themselves with other activities. After surgery this group showed the least emotional distress. They were described as cooperative and generally confident about their recovery.

Janis et al. explained the differences among these groups as due to differences in the ability to work through some of the feelings of threat and pain before they actually occurred. Some amount of worrying beforehand allowed the moderate group to feel reassured after surgery that things were going much as they had expected. Their recovery process was, in fact, confirmation of their own competence to test reality and therefore evidence that they were not really helpless or vulnerable to the whims of the medical staff or the hospital environment.

A further test of this concept involved giving additional information about postoperative pain to one group of surgical patients and omitting this information for the control group (Egbert, Battit, Welch, & Bartlett, 1964). The information included a description of the pain, reassurance that the pain was normal, techniques for relaxation that could relieve some of the pain, and information that medication for pain would be available as the patient needed it. After surgery the group that had been informed required significantly less pain medication. They were released from the hospital an average of 2.7 days earlier than the control group. During their hospital stay, they were rated by "blind" observation as in better emotional and physical condition than the controls. (In this kind of observation the observer does not know which patients are in the treatment group and which in the control group.) Janis et al. (1969, p. 105) offer this conclusion about the work of worrying: "A person will be better able to tolerate suffering and deprivation if he worries about it beforehand rather than remaining free from anticipatory fear by maintaining expectations of personal invulnerability."

The research we have discussed in this section emphasizes individual differences in the use of repression as a mechanism for minimizing stress. Repression is customarily defined as a defense mechanism in which anxiety-producing thoughts or wishes are lost to conscious awareness. An assumption is usually made that these thoughts are stored in the preconscious and continue to influence behavior without the person's knowledge. As we discuss below, the effectiveness of repression as a strategy for minimizing stress depends both on the person's ability to block out information and on the nature of the stressful situation. We might suggest that when the stressful situation includes opportunities to recover or to modify the conditions of stress, repression interferes with coping. When the stress is sudden and inalterable, then repression may in fact be adaptive.

Person/Environment Interaction

The process of coping is a product of the interaction of personal resources and preferred coping strategies with the demands or barriers of the situation. To understand coping, we must have a model of the relation between the person and the environment. Two approaches to this vital interface are described, one that provides a more global context for thinking about coping and one that examines the likelihood that particular coping strategies will be used under conditions of stress. The two models together bring us close to an appreciation of how people arrive at a coping strategy in the face of normative life crises or unpredicted life stress.

A General Model

The general model was developed by French, Rodgers, and Cobb (1974) in an effort to identify the basic components of adjustment. In this model there are two ways of defining the person. First, there is the objective person (Po) as he or she really is, according to objectively measured criteria for competences and needs. Second, there is the subjective person (Ps), or self-concept, which reflects the person's own perceptions of his or her competences and needs. The environment can also be viewed in two ways. The objective environment (Eo) includes the demands, resources, and barriers that exist independent of any person's perception or knowledge of it. The subjective environment (Es) is the environment as it is experienced and interpreted by the person.

The person's ability to accurately evaluate reality would be reflected in the difference between the objective and the subjective environment ($R = Eo - Es$). For example, a political candidate portrays himself as an upstanding, moral model when in fact he is having serious problems with his wife, drinking too much, and embezzling funds from the bank of which he is president. The voters perceive the candidate's worthiness on the basis of their subjective interpretations of his image as an upstanding, moral model. Only when the voters discover the information about the private life of the candidate will they recognize the discrepancy between their perceptions of him and the objective reality.

The person's ability to accurately assess the self, or self-insight, would be expressed as the difference between the objective and the subjective person ($A = Po - Ps$).

The concept of psychological stress is especially linked to the relation between Es and Ps. Whenever environmental resources are inadequate to meet the person's needs or when the person has inadequate competences to meet environmental demands, stress will result. The extent of the stress will be related to the accuracy of R (reality testing) and A (self-insight). In the case of our hypocritical politician, the lack of accuracy in R and A led to extended exposure to a stressful condition that had negative consequences for physical health.

In this model, coping can occur in at least four ways. To achieve a better match between personal needs and environmental demands, one of four components can be altered. First, the person can modify the objective environment, perhaps by bringing in additional resources, persuading someone to remove certain barriers, or shifting to a new environment. Second, the person can modify the objective person. This might include gaining new skills, using existing talents, entering into new relationships, or deciding to abandon certain motivations. Third, the person can alter the subjective environment. By projecting demands or barriers that do not exist, by minimizing the seriousness of an impending crisis, or by ignoring certain criteria for role performance, the person redefines the meaning of the environment. Finally, the person can alter the subjective person. Any of a number of defense mechanisms, including rationalization and repression, can change the person's perception of his or her own needs and thus diminish the discrepancy between environmental supply and personal motives. When changing perceptions of the self or the environment reflect objective changes, thus increasing the accuracy of R or A, the process is viewed as growth-producing. When subjective changes do not reflect objective changes, thus decreasing the accuracy of R or A, the process is viewed as maladaptive.

A Specific Model

Coping is any of a variety of strategies that have as their goal the reduction in the discrepancy between the person's needs and the environment's supplies. The second model looks in greater detail at the coping process as the person confronts stress. In this model, Janis and Mann (1976, p. 658) outline five patterns of coping that describe different strategies for responding to a stressful situation that calls for some kind of action. The five patterns are as follows:

1. *Unconflicted adherence.* The decision-maker complacently decides to continue whatever he has been doing, ignoring information about the risk of losses. A losing gambler continues to gamble even though the "house" has said more losing will lead to possession of home and car and garnishment of wages.
2. *Unconflicted change to a new course of action.* The decision-maker uncritically adopts whichever new course of action is most salient or most strongly recommended to him. The young college coed, interested in having sexual relations with a variety of partners, hears from her knowledgeable roommate that birth control pills are easy to take and very effective. Without asking the doctor about the dangers of this contraceptive, she begins to use them.
3. *Defensive avoidance.* The decision-maker evades the conflict by procrastinating, shifting responsibility to someone else, or constructing wishful rationalizations and remaining selectively inattentive to corrective information. A college student is on probation for poor grades but puts off studying for exams because the professor will be asking questions that are too difficult.
4. *Hypervigilance.* The decision-maker searches frantically for a way out of the dilemma and impulsively seizes upon a hastily contrived solution that seems to promise immediate relief, overlooking the full range of consequences of his choice because of emotional excitement, repetitive thinking, and cognitive constriction (manifested by reduction in immediate memory span and simplistic ideas). In its most extreme form, hypervigilance is referred to as "panic." A college student has been accused of cheating on an exam and may be thrown out of school. To avoid embarrassing and upsetting family

and friends, the student abruptly leaves the college in the middle of the night. No note or information of his whereabouts can be found. Family and friends become extremely worried and upset. In this instance, the student spares family and friends embarrassment, but has caused them a great deal of concern and worry.

5. *Vigilance.* The decision-maker searches painstakingly for relevant information, assimilates it in an unbiased manner, and appraises alternatives carefully before making a choice. Again, a college student has been caught cheating on an exam and is being dismissed. Rather than running away, this student decides on three alternatives. The first involves leaving the college and finding a job. The second involves approaching the professor who observed the cheating to work out a fair resolution. The third involves making an appointment with the dean of the college to ask for suggestions. After thinking of all the options, the student decides to contact the dean.*

It is probably obvious that in this model, although strategies 1 and 2 might be faster, only strategy 5 leads to well-developed choices. But in an immediate crisis that requires a rapid response, this last strategy might take too long. Similarly, if the threat of crisis does not materialize, then strategy 1 would be most effective.

The five coping strategies are each linked to the presence or absence of three environmental conditions. These conditions are part of the perceived environment. The best coping strategy depends on the perceived seriousness of any risks associated with action or inaction. It also reflects the hope or lack of hope of finding a solution. Finally, it reflects the person's perception about whether there is time to seek out additional information before a decision has to be made. If we could assume a totally rational problem solver, then each of the five coping strategies would represent an optimal response to a particular array of environmental conditions.

Figure 5-1 shows the relations among the three conditions of risk, hope, and time and the five coping strategies. As the figure suggests, the only coping strategy that results in a thorough consideration of the relevant information and the variety of options is vigilance. This strategy, in turn, is a product of three converging characteristics of the situation. Risk is entailed in both changing and not changing; there is hope of a bet-

* From "Coping With Decisional Conflict," by I. L. Janis and L. Mann, *American Scientist*, 1976, *64*(6), 657–667. Reprinted by permission of *American Scientist*, journal of Sigma Xi, The Scientific Research Society.

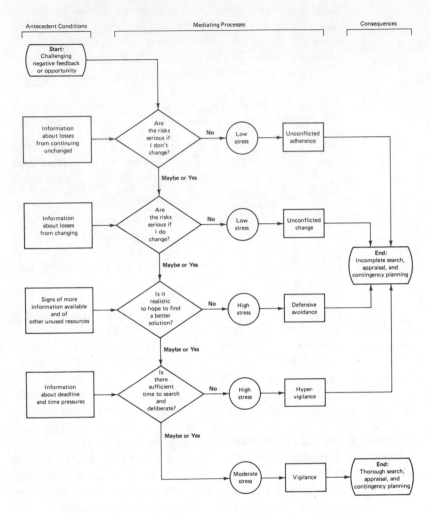

Figure 5–1.   Choice of a coping strategy. The conflict-theory
model of decision-making postulates that the way we cope with
resolving a difficult choice is determined by the presence or absence of three conditions: awareness of the risks involved, hope
of finding a better solution, and the time available in which to
make the decision. (From "Coping With Decisional Conflict,"
by I. L. Janis and L. Mann, *American Scientist,* 1976, *64*(6),
657–667. Reprinted by permission of *American Scientist,* journal of Sigma Xi, The Scientific Research Society.)

ter solution; and there is time to deliberate and to seek out additional information. All these environmental factors support an optimal coping
strategy. If the stress is too great or too little, the model predicts that effective coping will be limited.

Conclusions

Taking the two models together, we can draw the following conclusions about the coping process.

1. Coping will be determined by the person's tendency to try to
   alter the real environment, the real person, or the subjective
   assessment of the person or the environment. This tendency,
   though it may be partly determined by the nature of the situation, is also a product of the coping efforts of the past. Some
   people approach new crises with a view toward active mastery of the situation; others are more likely to blame short-
   comings in themselves for crises.
2. Coping will be determined by the stress of the situation.
   Some crises produce a prolonged state of tension. Solutions
   cannot be reached quickly, and there is no immediate demand for action. Other crises require a quick response. The
   time used for deliberation might lead to further danger. The
   most effective copers are able to modify their coping strategy
   to take into account the urgency of the situation.
3. In any situation, coping depends on the person's capacity to
   accurately assess both the situation and personal needs. At
   every life stage the resources for understanding the situation,
   for understanding personal needs, and for devising effective
   responses change. Coping competences show developmental
   change as well as personal stability.

Implications for a Life-Span Analysis
of Personality

The theme of crisis and coping raises once again the question of
stability and change in personality. The issue of change is implicit because
we assume that crisis provides an occasion for growth. If the person's existing resources and competences were adequate to reduce the stress of the
situation, it would not be a crisis. It is precisely the inadequacy of what we
might call the person's normal mode of functioning that makes crisis both
stressful and potentially growth-producing. From this perspective, the notion of normative crisis suggests a pattern of reintegration and expansion
throughout life. At every developmental stage we would expect a restructuring of the focus of personality that reflects the person's efforts to cope
with the psychosocial crisis of that stage. Further, the unpredictable crisis
events would offer additional challenges at every life stage that might be
met with adequate or ineffective coping efforts.

In general, we would expect coping skills to improve from childhood through adulthood. Increased cognitive skills, practice in coping

with stress, and the attainment of a sustaining personal philosophy should help the person to make increasingly accurate assessments of the situation and of his or her own needs. Of course, young children may make up in resilience what they lack in cognitive skills. Although they may not be able to plan out the most effective strategy or seek out additional information, they are also less burdened than adults by a sense of personal agency and memories of past crises. The complexity of roles and role expectations in adult life may make the consequences of crisis ever so much greater. What is more, the expectations for acceptable coping responses change with age. If a child strikes a teacher or bites another child in the class, that child might be disciplined, sent to the principal's office, or, at worst, suspended from school for a few days. If an angry teacher strikes a child, the teacher might lose his or her job. As one's coping competences increase, so does the complexity of the roles and responsibilities that must be maintained in the face of crisis.

Although crisis and coping generally are viewed as forces toward change, the notion of coping strategies or coping styles implies a stability in the preferred mode of responding. This stability is probably more evident in the ways people would like to respond than in the way they do respond to any given situation. Since situations have such different demand properties, the coping strategies that emerge are not very likely to look similar from one situation to the next. The stability in coping is most likely to be evident in the kinds of emotional responses that crisis tends to arouse, in the tendency to modify either the real or the subjective perception of person or environment, and in the person's general level of vulnerability to or insulation from stress. Evidence for these kinds of preferences for particular coping strategies has been the focus of this chapter.

The Type A and Type B behavior patterns described by Friedman and Rosenman (1974) are examples of this kind of stability. The Type A person shows "a chronic, incessant struggle to achieve more and more in less and less time, and is required to do so, against the opposing efforts of other things or other persons" (p. 13). The contrasting Type B person may be equally ambitious but is rarely harried or driven. Type B people approach situations with greater self-confidence and less hostility than Type A's. These patterns are viewed as response tendencies that will be evidenced mainly in the context of achievement-related demands or decision-making conflicts. Although the particular content of the behavior will differ from situation to situation, these orientations are described as stable characteristics of the person's coping strategy.

Perhaps the most perplexing question about crisis is the cumulative impact of life's trauma. How is it that some people are seemingly devastated by crisis and others rebound? How do we understand the tenacity and creative energy that is forged out of adversity for some and the cold, sullen suspiciousness that adversity brings to others? When we look back in the life histories of psychiatric patients, for example, we find no more evidence of crisis or trauma than in the life histories of a normal sample (Frank, 1965; Lazarus, 1976). The contribution of crisis to personality formation must be understood in light of the temperamental predispositions to respond to stress, the models for coping with stress who are present in the person's life, the timing and frequency of the stress events during the course of development, and the inner resources of the person that permit a creative restructuring of person/environment transactions during the crisis.

Chapter Six

Three Longitudinal
Studies of
Personality Development

In preceding chapters, we have considered four components of personality: temperament and talent, motives, roles, and coping styles. Each component contributes to the person's uniqueness. Each component also can be viewed from a developmental perspective, evolving through continuous interaction with the environment. In this chapter, we present three longitudinal studies that have struggled with the challenge of integrating the variety of variables that might be considered components of personality. The studies differ in the period of life they emphasize, in the variables that were measured, and in the origin of the sample. For these reasons they represent a variety of models for the longitudinal study of personality. The studies are similar in that they respect individuality and try to retain an appreciation of individual differences in the interpretation of the data. Each study also takes an optimistic stance about the potential for growth. A repeated theme is the centrality of coping to lifelong development. At every life stage, people are seen as actively contributing to their life histories. Although experiences, crisis, and resources definitely make an impact, the emphasis on coping draws our attention to the remarkable capacity to find meaning and purpose, to resolve conflict, and to continue to grow.

These studies tell us about the many faces of healthy development. They remind us that normal growth is not without its periods of turbulence and conflict. What looks like the precursor of lifelong turbulence may well be a transitional period of redefinition. Life events that might be viewed as a breeding ground for uncertainty and alienation can just as likely be a force for tempering and strengthening the person's commitment to self-fulfillment. We are cautioned to reserve judgment about the outcome of earlier patterns. As people move toward adulthood, a greater and greater diversity of life-styles emerges. At each developmental stage, the choices and opportunities that are present contribute to a divergence of lives.

Murphy's Studies of Vulnerability and Coping in Childhood and Early Adolescence

Coping is the process by which people use their inner resources, such as temperament and talent, to satisfy needs, to adapt to environmental demands, and to resolve stress. Coping includes gathering new information, maintaining control over one's emotions, and preserving freedom of movement. The following example serves as an illustration.

Colin was a 3-year-old boy in nursery school who had a wide range of interests, friendly, trusting relationships with adults, and cooperative, mildly aggressive relationships with classmates. He was characterized as having a great imagination, a large amount of energy, a great sense of optimism, and a large capacity to love. During his first year at nursery school, Colin seemed to sway between dependence and independence, controlling and not controlling aggression, and realizing and not realizing his body boundaries. When hugging a child, he hugged so vigorously that both would fall to the floor. Colin would then hold on until the other child showed some resistance. In the winter, Colin had chicken pox accompanied by an ear infection. Under the stress of the illness, Colin became more dependent on his mother and wanted to stay close to her all the time. He also stayed away from peers. Fortunately for Colin, he was able to recover from the stress by gathering his inner resources, such as abundant energy and optimism.

Lois Murphy has developed a longitudinal study of coping in childhood and early adolescence. Subjects were between 4 and 32 weeks of age during the first set of observations, made during the period 1948–1951 (Murphy & Moriarty, 1976). Infant observations included records of mother/infant interaction at feeding, play, and dressing. The babies were given developmental tests and pediatric examinations. Home interviews and a movie of feeding were also included.

During the preschool period, observations included parent interviews, pediatric examinations, psychiatric sessions, Miniature Life Toy (MLT) play sessions, parties, somatyping (assessment of body type using nude photographs), trips to the zoo, and "to-and-fro" reports describing the behavior of the child while traveling from home to the research setting. Among these observations the most stressful included separation from the mother to go with a stranger, the somatyping sessions, and the pediatric examinations. Observations about other life stresses, especially illness, loss of a loved one, or moving to a new town, were included through interviews and home visits.

During the period from 5 to 8, which Murphy called the Latency Study, the preschool observations and home interviews were repeated. To the initial battery were added the WISC (Wechsler Intelligence Scale for Children), the Rorschach, the Engel Insight Test, and the Witkin Perceptual Battery (a series of tests of field independence or field dependence). During this phase, the topic of stress was studied in greater depth. One mother kept a log of stressful events and the child's effort to cope with them. A small group of parents were interviewed about their perceptions of stress. Weekly play sessions were conducted with a child who was seriously disabled because of polio.

In early adolescence (11–13) another set of observations was made, including physical examinations, home visits, and psychological tests. A special study of the children's reactions to Kennedy's assassination was included, as well as intensive interviews following personal crisis in the lives of three of the subjects.

One has a sense that these subjects were just about as well known by a group of researchers as is possible given the distance in roles between scientist and subject. Using the rich set of both quantitative and interpretive observations, Murphy offers an analysis of several questions that have been central to the study of personality. First, she describes the origins of coping in infancy as they emerge in the mother/infant relationship. Second, she considers continuity and change in coping from infancy through early adolescence. Third, she considers the importance of individuality as it affects particular areas of vulnerability, resources for coping, and coping style. We will discuss some of Murphy's observations about each of these major themes.

The Origins of Coping in Infancy

Most mothers in the sample contributed significantly to the pattern of their children's development. Beginning in infancy, Murphy notes the ways that mothers stimulate their babies. Through physical and vocal contact, mothers are the primary determinants of the child's sensory world. Those babies who appeared to be the most developmentally advanced had frequent contact with their mothers and a stimulating home environment. Mothers responded to their babies' needs for interaction, for novelty, and for comfort as well as for food or sleep. Murphy suggests that responsiveness in the early phases of caregiving is central to the child's capacity for trust.

Some mothers were described as posing difficulties for their infants. One mother tended to overstimulate her baby, another mother teased hers, a third mother was both tense and rugged. In interactions with these mothers, babies experienced heightened frustration, distance, or uncertainty that seemed to persist in feelings of disappointment or hostility.

Generally, the mother/child relationship thrives most where the mother accepts the child's temperament and incorporates it into the pattern of mothering. Given individual differences in size, activity level, or sensory reactivity, the development of reciprocity emerged most fully when the mother could adjust her caregiving role in response to the child's needs. When reciprocity was high, Murphy found that the babies were most able to be absorbed in cognitive experiences, especially sensory exploration and problem-solving activities. The implication is that the baby's confidence in a responsive mothering relationship frees up energy for conceptual growth.

From the earliest point, the child also contributes to the emergence of a coping style. By no means totally passive, absorbent beings, infants impose their own direction to the care they receive. Babies with high energy and frequent vocalizations received more frequent facial and verbal expression from their mothers. Mothers of robust, healthy babies were more successful at breast feeding than mothers of smaller babies. Highly sensitive babies had mothers who were less successful at breast feeding. Babies who were active and expressive generally prompted greater responsiveness from their caregivers. Babies also chose to attend to certain stimuli rather than others. They preferred certain foods, toys, songs, and even people. During the second half of the first year, as their motor skills increased, they chose certain settings and expressed preferences for certain kinds of stimulation over others.

Finally, the emergence of a coping style in infancy was seen to be a product of the balance between gratification and challenge. Not every frustration or challenge was viewed as disruptive to growth. As Murphy looked back on the life histories of her subjects, she was able to identify challenges of infancy that prompted young infants to expand their efforts, to strive toward goals that might not be readily attainable. Some of these challenges appeared to have the potential for interfering with effective coping when they were first observed during infancy. However, from the perspective of development at adolescence, these same challenges appeared to have fostered unique strengths in some children. This is not to discount the possibility that some types of mothering may indeed interfere with the emergence of trust and autonomy. It merely emphasizes the possibility that children can transform some frustrations into opportunities for growth.

The challenges of infancy and their consequences can be illustrated by the interactions of one mother/infant pair in Murphy's study. The mother constantly teased her son by withdrawing objects of interest and placing them just beyond his reach. At first, Murphy interpreted this maternal interaction style as interfering with the infant's ability to develop an effective coping style. However, as the other mother/infant interaction styles were compared, Murphy hypothesized that this mother was actually providing challenges that encouraged her baby to overcome environmental obstructions. Thus, early in life these challenges prompted the baby boy to strive toward goals that were not readily attainable. Later in life, this boy continued to strive for goals that were not easily obtainable.

Continuity and Change from Infancy through Adolescence

Among the wide array of variables examined by other researchers in Murphy's study of coping and vulnerability, some dimensions appeared to be more continuous than others. Escalona (Escalona & Heider, 1959) predicted the pattern of preschool behaviors from infant observations. Areas in which predictions were frequently correct and those in which predictions were frequently incorrect are listed in Table 6–1. The

Table 6–1.   Prediction from Infancy to the Preschool Period

Frequently Correct Prediction Areas	*Frequently Incorrect Prediction Areas*
Motor coordination (pattern)	Response to the unfamiliar (new situations)
Motor development (maturation)	Shyness, response to strangers
Attention, concentration, involvement	Relationship with mother
Activity pattern and range	Basic attitudes and feelings regarding self and the world
Expressive behavior	Achievement needs, competitiveness
Perceptual sensitivity (intake)	Response to frustration (internal)
Intelligence level, pattern	Play style (thematic)
Affects (complexity, intensity, history)	
Decisiveness, goal striving	
Activity level	
Sex-role acceptance	
Sex-role conflicts (internal)	
Oedipal conflict, resolution, etc.	
Relationship to siblings	
Reaction of staff to child	
Interest pattern in play	
Interest pattern (excluding play)	
Fantasy, imaginativeness (intensity)	
Fantasy (quality, use of)	
Use of space (freedom in structuring of)	

importance of these lists is in identifying areas that are more and less vulnerable to the wide range of experiences that are confronted during the period from about 6 months to 3 years.

The question of continuity and change was addressed specifically by Heider (1966) in her assessment of the vulnerability, or susceptibility to distress, of children from infancy to the preschool period. Five children were judged *less* vulnerable at the preschool age than they were in infancy. These children benefited by physiological maturation that permitted greater resilience after the first 6 months. In contrast, 15 children became more vulnerable. Illness and mother's difficulties in adjustment, including depression, anxiety, or fatigue, appeared to account for this increase in vulnerability. Eleven children were rated as constant in their level of vulnerability, five continuing high, five continuing low, and one moderate.

One of the global characteristics of infancy, termed "functional stability," was a general absence of marked fluctuation in physiological responses, such as flushing or paling and perspiring, or variability in heart rate, blood pressure, or pulse. This measure in infancy correlated positively with three characteristics of the preschool child: (1) capacity for independence from the mother, (2) independence from the father, and (3) clarity of self-concept. Functional stability was negatively associated with anxiety.

Sensory reactivity, a general variable encompassing the infant's responsiveness to stimulation along all sensory dimensions, was associated with two components of social development for boys: rivalry and supportive peer relations. Sensory reactivity may make children more open to freer interaction and also more distressed by the intensity of stimulation from peers. In healthy children, sensory reactivity was generally associated with social and intellectual responsiveness.

Another area of continuity between the infancy and preschool periods was the relation between feeding behaviors and adaptive coping in the preschool setting. Behaviors described as "oral protest, resistance to disliked foods, and the ability to terminate feeding" were associated with a variety of variables that suggest the young child's capacity to control and regulate the impact of the environment. These early signs of willful selectivity in eating persisted in behaviors that showed the child's ability to impose his or her own structure on the environment.

A number of variables in infancy showed a positive correlation with aspects of functioning in early adolescence. Some surprising connections between infant variables and later coping style suggest the resilience of temperament and talent in shaping the pattern of subsequent encounters.

Age at sitting was correlated with variables that suggest both cognitive and social competences in early adolescence. These included clarity regarding own identity; social insight; preference for loosely structured situations; clarity of distinction between fantasy and reality; and intuitiveness (Murphy & Moriarty, 1976, p. 141). The baby who sits at an early age but does not walk early is able to observe much of the surrounding environment but must rely on others to satisfy needs. Murphy suggests that the opportunity to observe without action may facilitate the child's differentiation of self from others, eventually resulting in the cognitive and social competences of young adolescence. Sensory reactivity in infancy was associated with openness, curiosity, pleasure in tactile stimulation, and perceptiveness in social situations in early adolescence. This infant characteristic initiates a responsiveness to both the social and the physical environment that contributes to an effective coping orientation 12 or 13 years later. Thus, children who are open to environmental stimulation in infancy continue to react positively to sensory experiences in later childhood. These relationships are summarized in Table 6–2.

Surrounding this evidence for consistency is a context of change. For the sample as a whole, there were the expected changes in motor skills, in cognitive functioning, and in impulse control that helped to smooth out and integrate behavior from the preschool to the adolescent years. Within these general developmental changes, some children showed greater consistency than others. Moriarty (1966) analyzed the IQ scores of 65 children from infancy to preschool. Forty percent showed stable scores, 25% had increases in IQ, 9% showed a decline, and 26% had erratic scores. Similarly, Murphy (1976) described the patterns of coping styles from preschool to early adolescence. For 57% of the sample, coping style remained consistent across time. For the rest, there were clear changes in adaptive style and in general effectiveness. Variability can be present in maturity of different competences, in reactivity to environmental stimuli, or in ability to recover from stressful events. Murphy has identified the quality of variability as an essential component of some children's personalities. Whereas some children show a high degree of integration and stability of functioning, others evidence far less cohesiveness from situation to situation and from one developmental period to the next.

Individuality in Coping and Vulnerability

The dimensions of individuality are far too numerous to consider all of them. Here we can briefly identify a few of the characteristics of infant functioning that seemed to contribute most to the coping resources of infants and preschoolers in Murphy's study.

Activity level is a dimension that has several consequences for coping. The active child is in contact with a greater range of stimulation. Through exercise, the active baby also develops more coordinated motor routines that can be used to release tension or to manipulate objects. Quiet babies, in contrast, are less likely to expose themselves to overstimulation. They may have more opportunities to gaze and to listen.

Table 6–2. Continuity in Characteristics Observed in Infancy, Preschool Age, and Adolescence

Characteristics in Infancy	Characteristics at Preschool Age	Characteristics at Adolescence
Functional stability	Independence from father Independence from mother Clarity of self-concept Less anxiety	
Sensory reactivity	*Boys* Rivalry Supportive peer relations *Boys and Girls* Social and intellectual responsiveness	Openness Curiosity Pleasure in tactile stimulation Perceptiveness in social situations
Feeding behaviors (oral protest, resistance to dislike foods, ability to end feeding)	Ability to control and regulate environment, impose own structure on environment	
Age at sitting		Clarity regarding own identity Social insight Preference for loosely structured situations Clarity of distinction between fantasy and reality Intuitiveness

Sensory reactivity is another dimension of individuality that has consequences for coping. Children differ in maturation of the sense modalities, in sensitivity to stimulation in each modality, and in capacity to integrate information from each of the senses. The sensory stimuli that the infant finds pleasurable, whether they are a kind of tickling or roughhousing, a special song, a colorful toy, or a textured blanket, will guide caregivers in structuring the infant's environment. Babies who react negatively to hugging or tactile stimulation will probably not receive much of it. This does not mean that those babies do not need any intimate, loving interactions. However, they may respond in such a way that caregivers are likely to withdraw. Other studies have validated that the quality of the attachment differs according to the temperament of the infant and the responsiveness of the caregiver (Lewis & Rosenblum 1974; Schaffer & Emerson, 1964).

A third area of individuality that has consequences for coping includes the many kinds of vulnerability that exist in infancy. These include difficulties in digestion that produce gas pains, constipation, or frequent vomiting. Vulnerability can be experienced when certain stimuli are experienced as very painful. Some babies seem to lack the ability to modify stimulation. They are overwhelmed by the simultaneous input of sights, sounds, and activities, so that both eating and sleeping are repeatedly disturbed. The following description illustrates some of the ways that individuality is expressed through coping and some speculations on the long-term consequences of these early patterns.

> ... Consider Teddy at twenty weeks. He was also a baby with certain vegetative difficulties and sensitivity: periods of constipation and rectal adhesions with constipation may have caused pain; crying and feeding overlapped at times. Both some visual and auditory experiences seemed unpleasant—he did not like sunlight, and he became sober when lights were bright for photography. He "minded being wet or soiled more than many babies," and was "particular about the temperature and taste of foods." Tension was expressed through fretful vocalizations, a strained facial expression, flushing, postural tenseness with hands tightly fisted, loss of coordination, and loss of differentiation of vocalizations.
>
> At the same time he enjoyed many types of contact including fairly rough play with his father and was interested in observing objects.
>
> He could initiate pleasant experiences on his own, rubbing his face against the person who held him, making advances to his mother and also to staff members. He observed objects carefully before getting involved with them, and when he did become engaged with an object he maintained a fairly long attention span. In addition he showed far more ability than most babies of his age to initiate action to provide relief to his discomfort or tension.
>
> When he was bothered by the bright lights, he lowered his head, sucked a toy, then held his two hands, fingers interlaced, deep in his mouth.

When he became excited, then apprehensive, during the psychological test, he turned away from the examiner and faced his mother, relaxing and thus restoring his control.

With another period of tension, he swung himself back and forth on his mother's lap, stimulating her to resume rocking him.

Heider also felt that his interest in careful observation of features of the environment helped to reduce tension at times.

All together, then, Teddy was a sensitive baby who at the same time had many resources to restore stability and maintain integration in the face of disturbing experiences.

In line with his early vegetative difficulties, his response to severe stress (divorce of his parents when he was six years old) was to become obese. Turning away from and avoidance of disturbing stimuli at twenty weeks may be seen as precursors for later "forgetting" details of that stressful period. At the same time, his infantile perceptual and cognitive interests can be seen as precursors of his later intellectual competence in college. His early tactile and social responsiveness could be seen as a foundation for his later ease with people, and pleasant heterosexual relationships. He married early "a very sweet girl" [Murphy & Moriarty, 1976, pp. 86, 87].*

Vaillant's Study of Adult Life

The Grant Study began about 40 years ago in an attempt to understand the adaptive capacities of healthy, competent adults. Young men at a major Eastern university were selected according to the following criteria: (1) they met the requirements for college graduation; (2) they had no record of physical or psychological illness in their health-service record; (3) they were identified by the college deans as independent and "sound." From the 268 subjects in the original sample, Vaillant selected 95 for intensive interviews 30 years later. These men were in the classes 1942 to 1944 (Vaillant, 1977).

During the college years, about 20 hours were required of each subject. Data came from eight psychiatric interviews, a social history, a session at the home of each subject's parents, a two-hour physical exam, psychological tests, an electroencephalogram, and a somatotyping session by a physical anthropologist. Until 1955, the men were sent questionnaires annually. After that, questionnaires were sent every two years. These instruments focused on employment, family, health, habits, and political views. The men were all interviewed once in the period 1950–1952, and the subsample of 95 were interviewed again in the early 1970s. From

*From *Vulnerability, Coping, and Growth: From Infancy to Adolescence,* by L. B. Murphy and A. E. Moriarty. Copyright 1976 by Yale University Press. Reprinted by permission.

this pool of data, Vaillant addresses the course of adaptation. He describes the maturation of ego functions and the success or failure of negotiating the Eriksonian life crises of identity, intimacy, and generativity.

Perhaps the most significant contribution was Vaillant's developmental analysis of defensive styles. Figure 6–1 shows the percentage of vignettes (observed episodes of behavior) showing evidence of 15 defensive styles. Vaillant describes a maturing of defensive styles in middle adulthood that is characterized by more frequent use of sublimation, altruism,

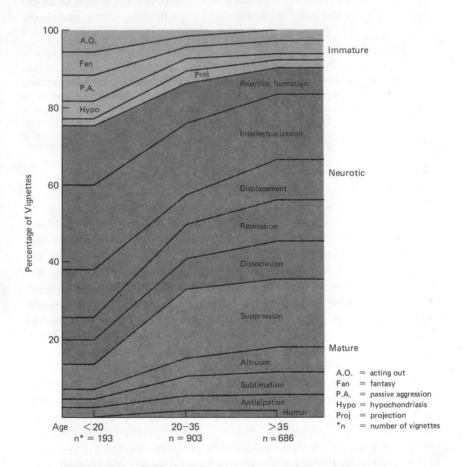

Figure 6–1. Shifts in defensive styles during the adult life cycle. This figure shows the proportion of vignettes that give evidence of immature, neurotic, and mature defenses at three age periods. (From *Adapation to Life,* by G.E. Vaillant. Copyright © 1977 by George E. Vaillant. Boston: Little, Brown and Company, 1977. Reprinted by permission of Little, Brown and Company.)

and suppression and declines in hypochondriasis, acting out, and fantasy. This maturity of defensive style results in a more productive, dependable life orientation. The pattern of maturation is even stronger if one separates the subjects who in adulthood achieved a sense of generativity, the capacity to contribute to the quality of life for future generations, from those who remained "perpetual boys." The latter group showed fewer immature defenses in adolescence. They took few risks and maintained an image of steady equilibrium. In adulthood, however, these steady adolescents appeared to be rocked by the greater intensity of adult challenges. The men who as adolescents appeared to be confused, impulsive, or angry were more likely to emerge in adulthood with a flexible, warm, and vigorous adaptive style.

Vaillant identifies factors within the person and factors in the environment that combine to support development toward a mature adaptive style in adulthood. Three inner factors contribute to adaptation. First, biological injury may result in temporary regression to a less mature adaptive style. The injury may call for greater distortion of one's view of reality, more impulsiveness, or greater dependency in relationships. Vaillant sees this regression as a potentially transitory shift that can be abandoned for a mature style once the injury is passed.

Second, adaptation reflects continued intellectual growth. Through experience, more complex analyses of events and a greater capacity to entertain multiple explanations of the same event emerge. Intellectual and ethical growth are fostered by participation in a variety of role relationships and by the demand to chart a life course using one's own problem-solving skills.

The third inner resource is the capacity to be involved in meaningful, loving relationships. Some part of this capacity depends on environmental supports; another element stems from the social competences and capacity for intimacy that the person brings into adult life. Over the life course, involvement in loving relationships and the need to experience intimacy increase. A deep investment in human relationships appears to be a component of health.

Three environmental factors contribute to adaptation. First, early experiences of loving relationships help children to bear pain, to anticipate positive outcomes, and to feel themselves worthy of love. Second, the array of adults, children, and heroic figures in the child's world provides the content for identification. Through this process, the values and strengths of significant others become internalized. People acquire new adaptive capacities by taking in some of the admired qualities of the target of identification. The defenses themselves were modeled by adults to whom the young men felt very close.

Third, the stresses and opportunities of the environment can promote or inhibit adaptation. The untimely death of a parent, rejection from a job, participation in military maneuvers involving the destruction of life are all examples of life events that bring intense stress. When a person is under stress, susceptibility to environmental influence is greater. The capacity to cope is directly influenced by the amount of environmental support available during stressful periods. It is much easier to appear to be coping in a mature manner when others admire you and support your personal growth. If the social environment is competitive or hostile, then periods of vulnerability may provoke additional attacks in order to demonstrate your limitations.

Vaillant argues that there is significant change during adulthood, both in the inner mechanisms of adaptation and in the observable behaviors defined as adjustment. Some adults emerge from a background of resources, opportunities, and parental encouragement to become restrained, depressed, and angry at others for their own failures. Others with far less support in childhood grab hold of opportunities and squeeze satisfaction out of each encounter. In general, the healthy members of the group became more involved with appreciating others and contributing to the lives of others. They showed a maturing religious commitment that integrated formal religious teaching with a caring, active moral orientation. There was continued redefinition of the parent/child relationship. The men rediscovered the strengths and weaknesses of their parents. They moved past the critical distance of their young adulthood or the idolization of early adolescence to a more complete appreciation of their parents as persons. Finally, healthy adaptation resulted in a vigorous engagement in life. In contrast to the self-absorption of adolescence or the guilt and depression of the thirties, after 45 the most successful Grant Study men showed a "celebration" of life.

Terman's Studies of the Gifted from Childhood through Adult Life

Terman's study of gifted children began in 1921 with the training of the research assistants and the identification of the sample. Elementary school teachers in the five largest cities in California were asked to nominate the two brightest children in their current class, the two brightest in the previous year's class, and the youngest child in the class. All the children who were nominated in each school were first given a group intelligence test. Those who tested over 140 were given the Stanford-Binet. If the children tested over 140 on the Stanford-Binet, their parents were asked for consent to have the child participate in the study. In this first sample, the youngest child in the class was more likely to be gifted than those nominated by the teacher (Seagoe, 1975). The final sample consisted of 1470 children with an average IQ of 151. Another group of 58 younger siblings was included in 1928.

Data collected from the sample in 1922 included "two intelligence tests, the four-hour Stanford Achievement Test, a general information test, seven character tests, a test of interest in and knowledge of play, thirty-four anthropometric measurements, a one-hour medical examination, a sixteen-page home information blank including ratings on twenty-five traits, a school information blank including similar trait ratings, an interest blank filled out by the child, a two-month reading record kept by the child, ratings on the socioeconomic status of the home, and a large amount of case history information supplied by teachers, parents, and field assistants" (Seagoe, 1975, p. 90).

It is important to recognize the social context of attitudes toward genius as a background for Terman's interest in these children. Some people believed that gifted children, especially those who showed unusual intelligence or talent in the toddler and preschool years, were freaks. People believed that these children were destined to be social isolates, that they would become insane, or that they would be unable to manage the normal challenges of everyday life. Other people resisted the idea of individual differences in intelligence. They argued that the public schools should provide equal education for all children and that all children had the same potential for learning. This argument was stated as an expression of the democratic ideal that all people are created equal and are entitled to equal rights and equal treatment under the law.

The gifted children represented every racial group in California. They came from homes of average or above-average socioeconomic status. Parents of the gifted were less likely to be separated or divorced and more likely to have completed high school than the general population.

Terman found that the gifted children were generally able to master the school curriculum two to four grades above their own. Most children were in grades two or three years below their mental age even though 85% had been accelerated at least once. In contrast to the view that gifted children are emotionally unstable, these children appeared to be honest, generous, and socially mature. Their social behavior was about average. Gifted children enjoyed games, including cards, chess, and checkers; they loved to read; and they were deeply involved in a variety of hobbies. Sex differences in play preferences and skill were less marked in this group than in the larger population.

Up to the time of Terman's death in 1956, four intensive field studies were conducted with the sample, in 1921 (the original data collection), 1927, 1939, and 1950. From 1940 through 1960, questionnaire data were collected every five years. The most recent follow-up study was conducted in 1972 by Robert Sears, whom Terman had asked to take responsibility for continuation of the research and management of the data.

The general question underlying subsequent studies was whether intellectual superiority would contribute to success in other life activities, especially in school, work, and family.

Over 80% of the males and females in the gifted group entered college. They were nearly two years younger than their classmates but were more likely than others to be active in student organizations, to receive honors, and to graduate with distinction. Two-thirds of the men and half the women continued their education after college to receive master's, Ph.D., or professional degrees (Seagoe, 1975; Terman, 1941).

Using the 1939 field study, Terman tried to identify the variables associated with occupational success. One of the most striking observations was how few women had pursued a career despite outstanding academic performance. Among the men, success was defined as the "extent to which each man was making use of his superior ability" (Seagoe, 1975, p. 97). For the men in the study,

> Terman found that the most successful group of gifted began to draw away from the least successful in the high school years, though differences in personality had been apparent even earlier. On maturity, the successful reported happier marriages, greater perseverance, more self-confidence, and less marked feelings of inferiority. They were rated superior in attractiveness, poise, speech, alertness, frankness, curiosity, and originality. They had much more often served as officers in World War II. Terman concluded that the difference between the relatively successful and unsuccessful gifted was largely determined by nonintellectual qualities such as social adjustment, emotional stability, and drive to accomplish. The one common denominator that appeared consistently among the successful was what Terman described as integration toward a goal [Seagoe, 1975, p. 97].

In 1972, the average age of the gifted sample was 62. Of six areas of life experience—family life, occupation, friendship, richness of cultural life, total service to society, and joy in living—family life was viewed as the most important and the one in which most satisfaction had been achieved. Among the men in the sample, satisfaction with work was more closely related to emotional variables, including optimism, enjoyment of work-related competition, and feelings of self-worth, than with objective criteria of success, such as income or occupational status (Sears, 1977). Satisfaction with family life in 1972 was associated with good mental health in 1940 and 1960, a score in the direction of feminine tastes and interests on the Strong Vocational Interest Blank in 1940, and admiration for one's father in 1950. Among the men in the sample, there was a negative relation between wife's income and husband's satisfaction with family life. The gifted group, who, by and large, did not show extreme sex-role stereotypy, experienced considerable strain in their late thirties and forties about enacting traditional sex-role expectations. By the fifties, this group expressed greater confidence in their own personal style and freedom from the constraints of narrow sex-role definitions (Sears & Barbee, 1978).

In addressing the question of stability and change, Sears (1977) made two important observations. First, among the gifted—and perhaps among other samples—prediction is best from one decade to the next. The strength of association decreases across longer spans of time. Therefore, we would not expect to find direct prediction from childhood variables to aspects of later adult life. Second, however, there are paths of association across the decades that are quite strong. Attitudes toward work, mental health, and a sense of satisfaction or self-worth show strong correlations from one time period to the next. This suggests that continuity is a characteristic of development, albeit tempered by the shifting pattern of competences and life challenges.

Comparison of the Three Research Programs

The research programs guided by Murphy, Vaillant, and Terman provide insight into the process of personality development in infancy and childhood, in adolescence and adulthood, and across the life span. Murphy and Vaillant emphasize intrapsychic processes, focusing on the evolution of adaptive strategies. Terman's work tends to highlight life outcomes, using the inner resource of intelligence as a selection variable. In Terman's study, the expression of intelligence in coping is not studied directly. Rather, it is assumed that this group has at its disposal the optimal capacity for coping with the full range of life events. Conversely, Murphy and Vaillant do not look in detail at the intellectual differences that might foster different coping patterns. None of their subjects are identified as intellectually exceptional, although all are described as in an above-average range.

In comparing the three studies, four points can be made about the process of personality development across the life span.

1. Each of the studies documents stability across life stages. In Murphy's work, this stability is seen in the continuity of such dimensions as activity level, orality, sensory reactivity, and smooth, integrated physiological functioning. These aspects of early infant coping become elaborated into more complex coping strategies during the preschool and preadolescent years. Terman emphasizes continuity of interests and talents. Intelligence itself remains a stable component of functioning that influences adaptation. What is more, among the gifted the development of social competences in adolescence has a continuing impact on satisfaction in work and family. Vaillant's study does not emphasize stability as much as maturation and growth. Nonetheless, the fact that Vaillant identifies characteristic adaptive styles or types implies an appreciation for the continuity in the use of defenses during adulthood. Especially among the "perpetual boys" there is predictability in the failure to develop a mature coping style.

2. Looking across life stages, both Murphy and Vaillant recog-

nize that some people are more likely to change than others. Some children appear to use the same strategies for coping with each new situation, while others are more responsive to the demands of the environment. In adulthood, some people continue to explore new strategies for coping, while others remain fixed on the patterns established in adolescence.

Reasons for using the same or more responsive strategies for coping with new situations seem to be related to parenting style, parental value systems, and sex. Moriarty and Toussieng (1976) completed the final phase of Murphy's study by examining the coping styles of adolescents. Two distinct groups were found. The Censors, a traditional group, kept established values and used a strategy for coping that restricted the impact of the environment. The Sensers, a group that emphasized renewal, used a coping strategy that investigated the environment. These two groups were broken down into subgroups on the basis of coping styles. The Censors were divided into the Obedient Traditionalists and the Ideological Conservatives. The Sensers were divided into the Cautious Modifiers and the Passionate Renewers. Table 6-3 identifies characteristics of these four groups.

Parenting style was related to the coping styles observed in all four groups. The Censors, both Obedient Traditionalists and Ideological Conservatives, had mothers who were controlling or distant and fathers who were physically or emotionally unavailable. Contrarily, both groups of the Sensers had close relationships with both parents. The parents' value system also influenced coping style. Both groups of the Censors and the Cautious Modifiers had parents with strong traditionalist views. The Passionate Renewers were more likely to have parents with less traditional views. Finally, sex of the adolescent was related to coping style. Of the Censors, 80% were boys, but only 41% of the Sensers were boys. The high percentage of boys in the Censor group may be related to the unavailability of the father. Thus, parenting style, parental values, and sex of the child may explain why some children appear to use the same strategies for coping with each new situation while others will explore new strategies for coping.

3. Adolescence appears to be a critical time for the consolidation of coping strategies and the direction of future growth. First, overcontrol during adolescence may prevent the kind of experimentation that is necessary in order to achieve the flexibility and perspective necessary for coping in adulthood. Second, interests and talents that are expressed during adolescence set a pattern for life choices that have long-range impact.

4. Amidst the many variables that were studied, a disconcertingly prominent one is the elusive energy or vitality that characterizes many subjects. In all the studies, a quality of optimism could be detected among certain subjects irrespective of the objective events of their lives. Some infants thrived in spite of ineffective mothering. Some adults felt energetic

Table 6–3. Characteristics of Censors and Sensers

Censors	Sensers
Obedient Traditionalists	*Cautious Modifiers*
—wholesome and free of guile	—distinct, vivid, usually socially poised
—express viewpoints and values most directly reflecting the traditional value system of their parents and their community	—have a decided interest in and compassion for people and all living things
	—retrospective and reflective by nature
—follow parental and religious standards because they feel they are right, comfortable, and an asset in establishing a reputation for moral decency	—curious about themselves and others, even those considered socially unacceptable
	—highly sensitive
	—appreciative of human individuality in what others do and believe
—do not question any of these standards or move out of the traditional to experience solely for the sake of experiencing	—cognizant of social inequities and hardships
	—seek to understand reasons for deviant behavior and protest
	—value parental opinions
Ideological Conservatives	*Passionate Renewers*
—impressively practical, organized, enterprising	—live dramatically and intensely
	—have relatively little concern for personal risks or social acceptability
—characteristically strive for self-improvement toward definite, high-level vocational goals	—seek and savor sensory experiences of all kinds
	—show originality in self-expression
—have predominantly traditional viewpoints about most topical issues	—have wide-ranging areas of interests
	—curious to the point of insistence
—define points of view more vigorously	—probe new ideas with considerable depth of feeling in their search for clarity
—pursue goals with more determination	—passionately enthusiastic
—often critical of others' points of view	—determined in pursuing a topic of immediate interest
	—willing to give free reign to their imagination
	—act boldly on their intuition
	—question established tradition

and proud of their life choices in the face of misfortune. Some of the most successful of the gifted were successful not so much because of their talents but because of the optimistic outlook they held of their lives. We infer from these observations that the self-concept is a central and essential element of personality. To fully appreciate the development of personality, one must understand the dynamic evolution of self-awareness. The self is a constant factor that integrates diverse experiences and interprets them in light of personal needs and goals. It is an inner reality that can dominate or redefine life events. As one of Vaillant's subjects wrote in a letter:

> "What's the difference between a guy who at his final conscious moments before death has a nostalgic grin on his face as if to say, 'Boy, I sure squeezed that lemon,' and the other man who fights for every last breath in an effort to turn time back to some nagging unfinished business?" [Vaillant, 1977, p. 357].

The answer to that question rests in the formulation of a sense of oneself—the topic of the next chapter.

Chapter Seven

The Development of a
Sense of Oneself

Still, my view is straightforward, namely, that man holds a variety of beliefs and theories about himself, some of which he is conscious of, some of which he is not; some of which are deeply repressed, some not salient enough to come beyond the subconscious, and others being the object of complete awareness. All of these are components of the theory, but only part is in conscious awareness. It takes only a brief stretch of imagination to see that in scientific theory generally, digging out the hidden assumptions, the unrecognized axioms and premises, the implicit and unsurfaced key propositions, is an integral part of the growth and development of science, as it is for individual human beings [Brim, 1976a, p. 244].

The Self-Concept

Let us begin our discussion of the self-concept by reviewing some of the highlights in theoretical contributions about a sense of self. Cooley (1902) commented on two components of a sense of self. One is the subjective experience that gives meaning to such statements as "I did it *myself*" or "That is *my* idea." It is an experience of control or a belief that control originates from within. The other component, the "looking-glass self," is the inferences about oneself that one draws from the ways that others react. One knows oneself to be attractive, successful, or interpersonally sensitive because of the responses of others. Mead (1934) expanded on this notion by describing the process of acquiring self-knowledge through interaction with others. In each of the roles we play, the self is discovered through the expectations others hold for our behavior. The reality of these expectations is very strong. Sullivan (1953) suggested that we even create a fantasy audience for whom we play out interactions. The notion that the self is discovered through interactions with the environment is central to Piaget's (1952) theory of cognitive development. Through exploration of objects and interactions with people, infants discover the boundaries of self as well as the properties of the environment. From these influences and others Epstein (1973) concluded that the self-concept is more aptly called a "self-theory."

> What is it that consists of concepts that are hierarchically organized and internally consistent; that assimilates knowledge, yet, itself, is an object of knowledge; that is dynamic, but must maintain a degree of stability; that is unified and differentiated at the same time; that is necessary for solving problems in the real world; and that is subject to sudden collapse, producing total disorganization when this occurs? The answer, by now, should be evident. In case it is not, I submit that the self-concept is a self-theory. It is a theory that the individual has unwittingly constructed about himself as an experiencing, functioning individual, and it is part of a broader theory which he holds with respect to his entire range of significant experience. Accordingly, there are major postulate systems for the nature of the world, for the nature of the self, and for their interaction. Like most theories, the self-theory is a conceptual tool for accomplishing a purpose. The *most fundamental purpose of the self-theory is to optimize the pleasure/pain balance of the individual over the course of a lifetime.* Two other basic functions, not unrelated to the first, are to *facilitate the maintenance of self-esteem,* and to *organize the data of experience in a manner that can be coped with effectively* [Epstein, 1973, p. 407].*

The theory about oneself draws on inner phenomena, such as dreams, emotions, thoughts, fantasies, and feelings of pleasure or pain. It also draws on the consequences of transactions with the environment. As with any set of concepts, the complexity and logic of the self-theory will depend on the maturation of cognitive functions. What is more, since the self-theory is based on personal experiences and observations, one would expect it to be modified by changing physical and socioemotional competences as well as by participation in new roles, all of which bring new content to the flow of experience. A brief description of the factors that may contribute to the self-theory at various stages of development will help provide the orientation of a life-span view of the sense of oneself.

Developmental Changes in the Self

At each stage, the self-theory is the result of the person's cognitive capacities and dominant motives as they come in contact with the stage-related expectations of the culture. In infancy, the self is primarily an awareness of one's independent existence. The infant discovers body

*From S. Epstein, The self-concept revisited; or, a theory of a theory. *American Psychologist,* 1973, *28,* 404–416.

boundaries, learns to identify recurring need states, and feels the comfort of loving contact with caregivers. These experiences are gradually integrated into a sense of the self as a permanent being existing in the context of a group of other permanent beings who either do or do not respond adequately to one's internal states.

In toddlerhood, the self-theory grows through an active process of self-differentiation. Children explore the limits of their capacities and the nature of their impact on others. Because of toddlers' inability to entertain abstract concepts and their tendency toward egocentrism, the perception of oneself as the center of the world, the child's self-theory is likely to depend on being competent and being loved. There is little concern about the perceptions of others, cultural norms, or future plans.

During early and middle school age, the child becomes more aware of the differences in perspective among people. An understanding of logical relations feeds into an appreciation of the concept of cultural norms. If one is in a certain role, one is expected to act in a certain way. The child is also aware of moral imperatives, which define good and evil. All these cognitive gains make the child more sensitive to social pressure, more likely to experience feelings of guilt or failure, and more preoccupied with issues of self-criticism and self-evaluation. At the same time, children between the ages of 5 and 12 remain relatively dependent on adults for material and emotional resources. Hence, self-esteem is likely to be most vulnerable during these years. Children continue to need reassurance about their competences and about being loved, although they are aware of external criteria for success that cannot be passed over with a hug and kiss from mother. They are also able to conceive of the future concretely enough to begin to worry about the kinds of responsibilities that will be expected of them as adults. The fact that they will have increased skills and resources to meet those future expectations may not be entirely obvious to children. Self-theory during these stages is based on children's evaluation of their skills, talents, and motivations, their ability to behave in accord with cultural norms, moral teachings, and role expectations, and their continued sense of love and acceptance from significant others.

The self-theory is crystallized during later adolescence. As young people establish a sense of autonomy from their parents, they begin a process of reviewing and evaluating their childhood skills, values, and goals. Because of their increased conceptual complexity and emotional autonomy, they are able to organize their self-theory around a set of values, goals, and competences that are more relevant to their personal temperament and to the current cultural reality that they confront. The anxiety and tension surrounding the crisis of identity are the result of a conceptual and emotional separation from many of the attractions of childhood and a commitment to a view of oneself as persisting in a future that is largely unknown. If a personal identity can actually be achieved at this stage, then the self becomes much more of a directing, integrating structure that moves the person toward future goals.

Once identity is achieved, the self becomes an autonomous structure. Adults can undergo extreme stress and still manage to preserve a sense of their personal motives and goals. They can perform roles that are unpleasant, meaningless, or humiliating and still isolate a part of their self-concept from these negative experiences. The self is protected by the formation of an integrated, abstract value system that has meaning, regardless of daily events. Nevertheless, as adults perform new roles in which they invest energy, the content of the self expands to incorporate new areas of skill development, new sources of personal satisfaction, and modifications in values and beliefs.

In later adulthood the process of introspection brings renewed attention to the components of the self-theory. Although the adult may experience some shift in orientation and in priorities during this stage, we suggest that the content of the self-concept remains rather stable. It is the evaluative component of the self that fluctuates during this stage. As adults first approach the tasks of developing a point of view about death and accepting their own past life, they are likely to experience some severe feelings of depression and lack of worth. They cannot change the direction they have pursued throughout their adult years, and they may feel regret about it. As they become more resigned to their past, their self-esteem will rise. With extreme age there is at least a fantasy in the mind of the theorist that the process of self-differentiation that began in birth shifts to a gradual process of self-integration. In that process, people may attend less to the differences between themselves and others and more to the similarities. Because of their perspective on time, very old people can have a greater ability to identify with people of other ethnic groups, other historical periods, and other cultures. In the aging process, the self can become linked with the rest of humanity.

We have offered a view of the self-theory as acquiring new attributes at each developmental stage. Every new competence, every new role relationship, every encounter with novel historical events has the potential for bringing about revisions in the self-theory. At any single moment, however, the self-theory serves as an internal anchor point for assessing external events and preparing for future activities.

Turner (1976; Turner & Gordon, 1978) has followed up on a common observation that leads us toward a new understanding of the self. He suggests that the self is allied to some set of experiences and that the range of these experiences constitutes the boundaries for the authentic self. When we feel ill at ease, phony, or self-conscious, we are responding to some discrepancy between the realm of events occurring around us and the realm that has been identified as authentic. It is not clear exactly what realm of experiences becomes encompassed by the self—that is, why some experiences seem authentic and others seem alien. Turner has suggested a categorization system along two dimensions. The authentic self can be tied to experiences in institutional settings or to experiences that originate from inner feelings and fantasies. The second dimension is a distinction between experiences with others and experiences alone. One could also imagine the primary experiences of self tied to particular periods of development. In other words, some people recall the events of the early school years as most authentic, while others recognize adolescence as a time of primary relevance. The point is that the self is bounded by the experiences and concepts that are applied to it. This is really what is meant by the term *subjectivity*. Every person takes his or her authentic self as the senser into each new experience. The self, defined as it is by the convergence of what is viewed as authentic, pleasurable, and desirable, screens each experience for its meaning, relevance, and benefit. The difference between what is described as the subjective reality and the objective reality is the difference between those experiences and concepts that are shared by many people and can therefore reach consensus and those that are of heightened and idiosyncratic importance to a particular person. In this sense, the self may be experienced as unique and yet share many characteristics with the self-theories of others. Interestingly, people tend to identify the self with those characteristics that are highlighted by their uniqueness. Rather than appreciating all the things one shares with others, one defines the self by those aspects that are perceived as uncommon or special. If one asked a large group of people to describe themselves, it would not be surprising if 80% of the respondents described themselves as "unique."

The sense of oneself is not identical to personality. Rather, personality is the larger configuration of temperament, talents, motives, and roles. The self is a focusing, integrating construct that may not be aware of or responsive to every component of personality. That is why the term *self-insight* or *consciousness* makes sense. The sense of self may encompass a broad range of personality characteristics, or it may be limited to certain "acceptable" qualities. The person may not have the concepts to apply to the characteristics of the self that could be objectively observed or measured by others. For example, we believe that the choice of defense mechanisms is a major characteristic of personality. One's sense of self may or may not include an awareness of one's defensive style, depending on whether or not one knows about defense mechanisms and observes their functioning in ongoing interactions. This does not mean that only those people who recognize defenses as a component of self actually use these mechanisms.

If we think of the sense of oneself as a theory, then we recognize the continuous possibility for change. One begins with some identifiable experiences. They may be feelings of pain or pleasure, recognition of one's physical appearance, or predictable patterns of responses that others make toward one. From these pieces of evidence, one draws a variety of inferences about one's essential character. Younger children tend to draw inferences about more specific, concrete characteristics, such as age, sex, or associations. Older children and young adults begin to draw inferences about values and personal qualities. Just as an infant's mental image of a permanent object evolves in steps through repeated exploration of objects in space and repeated experiences of the departure and return of persons and objects, so one's image of oneself evolves through assimilation and accommodation. (In the process of assimilation, people incorporate new experiences with objects and others by emphasizing similarities between these new experiences and the existing sense of self. In the process of accommodation, they change their existing sense of self to account for novel elements in experiences with objects and others. In this process, novelty is gradually blended into the self-concept, adding confirmation of some familiar and constant dimensions as well as reshaping some dimensions in new directions.) Each encounter verifies some aspects of the theory or calls it into question. At each life stage the self-theory is revised owing to new information and new interactions.

At some point, however, the theory of oneself takes on a more active role in guiding life events. Perhaps it is most appropriate to think of that point as the achievement of identity. However, there is evidence that it occurs even before later adolescence. By the fourth grade, children who have a history of school failure begin to diverge in their assessment of their own ability from children who have a history of school success (Kifer, 1978). This assessment will contribute to an optimistic or pessimistic view about the likelihood of future success. It will influence the choice of peer relationships, the confidence one brings to new tasks, and the formulation of future aspirations.

By later adolescence, the crystallization of a personal identity represents an attempt to spell out more explicitly the elements of one's self-theory. It is an attempt to clarify personal goals and commitments and to tie them to one's sense of past history as well as ongoing achievements. Once a personal identity is achieved, it serves in a highly active manner, guiding the selection of career, articulating a moral code, and directing one's decisions about marriage, religion, and political commitments.

Self-Esteem

For every component of the self—the physical self, the self as reflected in others' behavior, or the array of personal aspirations and goals—the person makes an evaluation of the worthiness of that characteristic. This self-evaluation, or self-esteem, is based on two essential sources: (1) the comparison between achievements and expectations and (2) messages of love, support, and approval from others. Feelings of being loved, being valued, being admired, or being successful contribute to a sense of worth. Feelings of being ignored, rejected, scorned, or inadequate contribute to a sense of worthlessness. Self-esteem can be altered when one succeeds or fails at an important task. It can be enhanced through positive responses from important others and diminished by negative responses. By adulthood, however, one has a pervasive sentiment about one's worth that sets the tone of optimism or pessimism about future life events. The level of self-esteem contributes to the willingness to take risks, to expectations about success or failure, and to the expectation that one will have a meaningful impact on others.

Studies that evaluate the impact of success and failure on self-esteem illustrate the power of this evaluative component of the self-theory in interpreting life experiences. First, there are studies that consider the impact of experimentally induced success or failure or of false feedback about success or failure on self-evaluation. Subjects might receive false scores on a test, be asked to solve impossible tasks, or be told that tasks that in reality are extremely difficult are well within the normal range for a person of the subject's age (Archibald & Cohen, 1971; Rule & Rehill, 1970; Zellner, 1970). The consequences of these experimental manipulations depend on at least two important factors. First, the experience of failure has a greater negative effect on self-evaluation if the skill or competence was one that the subject viewed as important and central to the self-concept. Failure at a task in an unimportant area of competence does not require the same reassessment of personal worth as failure in an area that the person judges to be a well-developed talent (Newman & Newman, 1979). Second, failure messages tend to depress the self-esteem of people who have a low or medium level of self-esteem to begin with. People with high self-esteem do not tend to be as negatively influenced by failures. In this sense, feelings of self-worth provide a protective shield around the self. If the person holds a positive, optimistic self-evaluation, then negative messages incongruent with that self-evaluation are deflected. The person with high self-esteem will explain failures by examining the task, the amount of time to work, the other people involved, or the criteria for evaluating success and failure. In contrast, the person with low self-esteem will see the failure as another bit of evidence about his or her lack of worth (Wells & Marwell, 1976).

A second approach to the study of the effect of success or failure is described by Rosenfeld (1978). Instead of manipulating feedback about successes and failures, Rosenfeld trained sixth-grade students to recall and report their daily school-time successes and failures. One group was asked to report successes for 20 school days, another group to report failures, and a third group to report their teacher's successes. Each strategy had a different impact on the high- and low-self-esteem students. The only group that benefited from recalling successes was the group with initially high self-esteem. Low-self-esteem students showed greater movement toward a positive evaluation when they reported their own failures or the teacher's successes. Reporting failures led to decreased esteem for the high-self-esteem students but not for the low-self-esteem students. This intervention demonstrates two characteristics of the self-concept. First, it is possible to influence one's self-evaluation by drawing attention to some particular set of behaviors and ignoring others. Second, the enhancing effect of emphasizing successes is dependent on the pattern of successes or failures among other members of the group. If one child sees that he or she has considerably fewer successes than the other children in the class, emphasizing successes appears to have the effect of emphasizing a deficit.

Perhaps the most troublesome fact is that self-esteem is not directly tied to any objective measures of life success. Campbell (1976; Campbell, Converse, & Rodgers, 1976) has begun to evaluate the correlates of a subjective sense of well-being. Well-being, as he measures it, can be thought of as an estimate of self-esteem. He looked at the joint contribution of ten variables: sex, religion, education, occupation of head of household, family income, being employed or unemployed, race, age, urban or rural community, and phase in the life cycle (married, parenting, widowed, and so forth). All these variables together accounted for less than 20% of the variance in life satisfaction, positive or negative feelings about life experiences, or perceptions of stress. The variable that was most highly correlated with life satisfaction was the life-cycle dimension. Among the groups with high satisfaction were young, married females with no children, married males over 30 with no children, and married males and females with children over age 17. Those who experienced the highest stress were divorced or separated females and married couples with children under 6. Sex differences also converge with life phase to determine feelings of satisfaction and stress. Being young and unmarried is more stressful for females than males. Being over 30 and single is associated with more negative, unpleasant feelings for males than for females. In general, being married is associated with greater life satisfaction than being single. Interestingly, being widowed is associated with far less stress than having children under age 18.

Life satisfaction is not clearly tied to objectively measurable factors. It may well be a conceptual invention that is imposed on life events by most people. This invention is crafted out of the overall match between personal expectations, or standards, for success and the extent to which past accomplishments have met these standards (Bandura, 1977). In adulthood, one of the functions of the self-concept is to achieve a sense of satisfaction with the life course as it has evolved, taking pleasure in one's achievements and modifying disappointments with a philosophical sense of acceptance.

The Relation of a Sense of Oneself to Personality

We have already suggested that the sense of oneself, though a critical element in the personality, does not encompass all the components of personality. At any life stage, the sense of oneself highlights only a subset of the details of the complex tapestry of personality. In this section we look back on the themes that have been raised in preceding chapters and ask how each element contributes to the sense of oneself.

Temperament is an early component of personality that both regulates and provokes interactions. As relatively stable components of early childhood, temperamental characteristics come to be labeled and recognized as descriptive of the person. Children are described as active, bright, fussy, or sociable—to name only a few temperamental qualities. These characteristics help adults create experiences that will be pleasurable for the child. Even though the labels for these qualities are not applied by the young child to describe the self, they emerge by the end of the elementary school years (sixth grade) as an essential element of selfhood (Montemayor & Eisen, 1977).

Talents, the specific areas of competence, are recognizable at a young age. They are especially central to the sense of oneself because they usually reflect areas of uniqueness. Against the background of the many people one encounters, what makes each one stand out? A talent is a readily identifiable characteristic that each person can claim as evidence of his or her individuality. A talent that is identified will, of course, be influenced by the readiness of others to recognize that talent and by the opportunities in the environment to exercise it. Especially in early childhood, when life roles and values are less prominent, the sense of oneself is heavily influenced by the person's experiences with special areas of competence.

Motives are part of the sense of oneself to the extent that the person recognizes certain personal needs and goals. When people describe themselves as "needing to be loved" or "needing to win," they are articulating an awareness of their motives. As motives change, the sense of oneself is modified in order to more accurately predict what is satisfying or desired and what is not. Not all motives are recognized as influencing behavior. In fact, the notion of defense mechanisms suggests that people do not claim ownership of all motives. For example, a person may perceive himself or herself as loving and cooperative and at the same time project hostile feelings onto others. A component of personality—hostility—is then not included in the sense of oneself. The sense of self may include motives that one deems undesirable, such as being too much in need of approval or too anxious about failure. Some motives, however, are excluded from the self-theory but still continue to influence behavior.

Social roles dominate the sense of oneself for some people. Especially in adulthood, family and work roles require so much time, thought, and energy that they can easily assume a central role in the process of self-definition. However, since the role of worker, parent, husband, or wife is shared with many people, it is, once again, the unique enactment of these roles that is most readily incorporated into the sense of self. Either the special strategies for meeting expectations or the particular areas of vulnerability and incompetence are highlighted.

Crisis and the process of coping alert us to a final and vital element in the formulation of a sense of oneself. Lest we tend to overemphasize the conceptual dimensions of selfhood, our perceptions, attributions, and expectations for self and others, the concept of coping reminds us of the vigorous, tenacious striving for survival and growth that is essential to human experience. The sense of self can be limited by the boundaries of institutional and cultural roles or norms, but it need not be. As one copes with crisis, one recognizes the possibility of overcoming or dominating the configuration of events by creating new solutions. Coping requires the imposition of self to redefine experience. Through repeated experiences of successfully coping with stress, one begins to perceive oneself as a continuously expanding entity, increasing in self-awareness and knowledge of the environment with each life experience. The more one recognizes the limitations of one's own subjective perspective, the more one's sense of self can reach beyond the limits of that subjectivity. The sense of oneself comes to embody a life history of experiences that emerges as a factor, no matter how small, in the shaping of subsequent life events.

References

Adler, A. *Social interest: A challenge to mankind.* New York: Putnam, 1964. (Originally published, 1939.)

Albert, R. S. Toward a behavioral definition of genius. *American Psychologist,* 1975, *30,* 140–151.

Allport, G. W. *Personality: A psychological interpretation.* New York: Holt, 1937.

Allport, G. W. *Becoming: Basic considerations for a psychology of personality.* New Haven, Conn.: Yale University Press, 1955.

Allport, G. W. *Pattern and growth in personality.* New York: Holt, Rinehart & Winston, 1961.

Allport, G. W. *The person in psychology.* Boston: Beacon Press, 1968. (a)

Allport, G. W. Personality: Contemporary viewpoints (I). In D. Sills (Ed.), *International encyclopedia of the social sciences.* New York: Macmillan, 1968. (b)

Angelino, H. R. Sex and aging. Paper presented at the 85th annual meeting of the American Psychological Association, San Francisco, August 26–30, 1977.

Archibald, W., & Cohen, R. Self-presentation, embarrassment, and facework as a function of self-evaluation, conditions of self-presentation, and feedback from others. *Journal of Personality and Social Psychology,* 1971, *20,* 287–297.

Astin, A. W. *Four critical years.* San Francisco: Jossey-Bass, 1977.

Atkinson, J. W., & Birch, D. *Introduction to motivation* (2nd ed.). New York: Van Nostrand, 1978.

Atkinson, J. W., Heyns, R. W., & Veroff, J. The effect of experimental arousal of the affiliation motive on thematic apperception. *Journal of Abnormal and Social Psychology,* 1954, *49,* 405–410.

Atkinson, J. W., & Raynor, J. *Motivation and achievement.* Washington, D.C.: V. H. Winston and Sons, 1974.

Ban, P., & Lewis, M. Mothers and fathers, girls and boys: Attachment behavior in the one-year-old. *Merrill-Palmer Quarterly,* 1974, *20,* 195–204.

Bandura, A. *Social learning theory.* Englewood Cliffs, N.J.: Prentice-Hall, 1977.

Barker, R. G., & Gump, P. V. *Big school, small school: High school size and student behavior.* Stanford, Calif.: Stanford University Press, 1964.

Barker, R. G., & Schoggen, P. *Qualities of community life: Methods of measuring environment and behavior applied to an American and an English town.* San Francisco: Jossey-Bass, 1973.

Baumrind, D. Current patterns of parental authority. *Developmental Psychology Monographs,* 1971, *4,* 99–103.

Biddle, B. J., & Thomas, E. J. *Role theory: Concepts and research.* New York: Wiley, 1966.

Birch, D., Atkinson, J. W., & Bongort, K. Cognitive control of action. In B. Weiner (Ed.), *Cognitive views of human motivation.* New York: Academic Press, 1974.

Block, J. *Lives through time.* Berkeley, Calif.: Bancroft Books, 1971.

Brim, O. G., Jr. Socialization through the life cycle. In O. G. Brim, Jr., & S. Wheeler (Eds.), *Socialization after childhood: Two essays.* New York: Wiley, 1966.

Brim, O. G., Jr. Adult socialization. In J. Clausen (Ed.), *Socialization and society.* Boston: Little, Brown, 1968.

Brim, O. G., Jr. Life-span development of the theory of oneself: Implications for child development. In H. W. Reese (Ed.), *Advances in child development and behavior* (Vol. 11). New York: Academic Press, 1976. (a)

Brim, O. G., Jr. Theories of the male mid-life crisis. *Counseling Adults,* 1976, *6,* 2–9. (b)

Bronson, W. C. Adult derivations of emotional expressiveness and reactivity-control: Developmental continuities from childhood to adulthood. *Child Development,* 1967, *38,* 801–817.

Brown, R. *Social psychology.* New York: Free Press, 1965.

Buss, A. H., & Plomin, R. A. *A temperament theory of personality development.* New York: Wiley, 1975.

Campbell, A. Subjective measures of well-being. *American Psychologist,* 1976, *31,* 117–125.

Campbell, A., Converse, P. E., & Rodgers, W. L. *The quality of American life.* New York: Russell Sage Foundation, 1976.

Cartwright, L. K. Career satisfaction and role harmony in a sample of young women physicians. *Journal of Vocational Behavior,* 1978, *12,* no. 2, 184–195.

Cattell, R. B. *Personality and motivation: Structure and measurement.* New York: Harcourt Brace Jovanovich, 1957.

Cattell, R. B. *The scientific analysis of personality.* Chicago: Aldine, 1966.

Cattell, R. B. *Personality and mood by questionnaire.* San Francisco: Jossey-Bass, 1973.

Caudill, H. M, *Night comes to the Cumberlands: A biography of a depressed area.* Boston: Little, Brown, 1962.

Chess, S., & Thomas, A. Temperament in the normal infant. In J. C. Westman (Ed.), *Individual differences in children.* New York: Wiley-Interscience, 1973.

Chiang, H. M., & Maslow, A. H. *The healthy personality.* New York: Van Nostrand, 1977.

Chwast, J. Sociopathic behavior in children. In B. B. Wolman (Ed.), *Manual of child psychopathology.* New York: McGraw-Hill, 1972.

Condry, J., & Dyer, S. Fear of success: Attribution of cause to the victim. *Journal of Social Issues,* 1976, *32,* 63–83.

Cooley, C. H. *Human nature and the social order.* New York: Scribner's, 1902.

Cortes, J. O. A comprehensive model of career development in early childhood. *Journal of Vocational Behavior,* 1976, *9,* 105–118.

Coser, R. L., & Rokoff, G. Women in the occupational world. *Social Problems,* 1971, *18,* 535–554.

Crowne, D. P., & Marlowe, D. A new scale of social desirability independent of psychopathology. *Journal of Consulting Psychology,* 1960, *24,* 349–354.

Cumming, E., & Henry, W. E. *Growing old: The process of disengagement.* New York: Basic Books, 1961.

Darley, S. Big-time careers for the little woman: A dual-role dilemma. *Journal of Social Issues,* 1976, *32,* 85–98.

Datan, N., & Rodeheaver, D. Dirty old women: Emergence of the sensuous grandmother. Paper presented at the 85th annual meeting of the American Psychological Association, San Francisco, August 26–30, 1977.

de Beauvoir, S. Joie de vivre. *Harper's,* January 1972.

Dellas, M., & Gaier, E. L. Identification of creativity: The individual. *Psychological Bulletin,* 1970, *73,* 55–73.

Edgerton, R. B. "Cultural" vs. "ecological" factors in the expression of values, attitudes, and personality characteristics. *American Anthropologist,* 1965, *67,* 442–447.

Edwards, A. L. *The social desirability variable in personality assessment and research.* New York: Dryden, 1957.

Egbert, L., Battit, G., Welch, C., & Bartlett, M. Reduction of postoperative pain by encouragement and instruction of patients. *New England Journal of Medicine,* 1964, *270,* 825–827.

Epstein, S. The self-concept revisited; or, a theory of a theory. *American Psychologist,* 1973, *28,* 404–416.

Erikson, E. H. *Childhood and society.* New York: Norton, 1950.

Erikson, E. H. Growth and crisis of the healthy personality. *Psychological Issues, 1* (1), Monograph 1, 1959, 50–100.

Escalona, S. K., & Heider, G. M. *Prediction and outcome: A study in child development.* New York: Basic Books, 1959.

Eysenck, H. J. *The biological basis of personality.* Springfield, Ill.: Charles C Thomas, 1967.

Feld, S. C. Longitudinal study of the origins of achievement strivings. *Journal of Personality and Social Psychology,* 1967, *7,* 408–414.

Fiske, D. W. *Strategies for personality research: The observation versus interpretation of behavior.* San Francisco: Jossey-Bass, 1978.

Flanagan, J. C. A research approach to improving our quality of life. *American Psychologist,* 1978, *33,* 138–147.

Flerx, V. C., Fidler, D. S., & Rogers, R. W. Sex-role stereotypes: Developmental aspects and early intervention. *Child Development,* 1976, *47,* 998–1008.

Frank, G. H. The role of the family in the development of psychopathology. *Psychological Bulletin,* 1965, *64,* 191–205.

French, J. R. R., Rodgers, W., & Cobb, S. Adjustment as person-environment fit. In G. V. Coelheo, D. A. Hamburg, & J. E. Adams (Eds.), *Coping and adaptation.* New York: Basic Books, 1974.

Freud, A. *The ego and the mechanisms of defense.* New York: International Universities Press, 1936.

Freud, S. Three essays on the theory of sexuality. In J. Strachey (Ed.), *The standard edition of the complete psychological works of Sigmund Freud* (Vol. 7). London: Hogarth, 1953. (Originally published, 1905.)

Freud, S. Introductory lectures on psychoanalysis. In J. Strachey (Ed.), *The standard edition of the complete psychological works of Sigmund Freud* (Vols. 15 and 16). London: Hogarth, 1963. (Originally published, 1917.)

Freud, S. New introductory lectures on psychoanalysis. In J. Strachey (Ed.),

The standard edition of the complete psychological works of Sigmund Freud (Vol. 22). London: Hogarth, 1964. (Originally published, 1933.)

Friedman, M., & Rosenman, R. H. *Type A behavior and your heart*. New York: Knopf, 1974.

Gamer, E., Thomas, J., & Kendall, D. Determinants of friendships across the life span. In F. Rebelsky (Ed.), *Life: The continuous process*. New York: Knopf, 1975.

Gecas, V. The socialization and child care roles. In F. I. Nye (Ed.), *Role structure and analysis of the family*. Beverly Hills, Calif.: Sage Publications, 1976.

Getzels, J. W., & Jackson, P. W. *Creativity and intelligence: Explorations with gifted students*. New York: Wiley, 1962.

Goertzel, V., & Goertzel, M. G. *Cradles of eminence*. Boston: Little, Brown, 1962.

Guilford, J. P. *The nature of human intelligence*. New York: McGraw-Hill, 1967.

Gutmann, D. The country of old men: Cross-cultural studies in the psychology of later life. Occasional Papers in Gerontology, No. 5. Ann Arbor: Institute of Gerontology, University of Michigan/Wayne State University, 1969.

Gutmann, D. Alternatives to disengagement: The old men of the highland Druze. In R. LeVine (Ed.), *Culture and personality: Contemporary readings*. Chicago: Aldine, 1974.

Gutmann, D. Parenthood: A key to the comparative study of the life cycle. In N. Datan & L. H. Ginsberg (Eds.), *Life-span developmental psychology: Normative life crises*. New York: Academic Press, 1975.

Hall, C. S., & Lindzey, G. *Theories of personality* (3rd ed.). New York: Wiley, 1978.

Hamlin, R. M. Restrictions on the competent aged. Paper presented at the 85th annual meeting of the American Psychological Association, San Francisco, August 26–30, 1977.

Hanley, C. Physique and reputation of junior high school boys. In M. C. Jones, N. Bayley, J. W. Macfarlane, & M. P. Honzik (Eds.), *The course of human development*. Waltham, Mass.: Xerox College Publishing, 1971.

Harmon, L. W. The childhood and adolescent career plans of college women. *Journal of Vocational Behavior*, 1971, *1*, 45–56.

Harter, S. Effectance motivation reconsidered: Toward a developmental model. *Human Development*, 1978, *21* (1), 34–64.

Havighurst, R. J. Youth in exploration and man emergent. In H. Borrow (Ed.), *Man in a world at work*. Boston: Houghton Mifflin, 1964.

Havighurst, R. J., Neugarten, B., & Tobin, S. S. Disengagement and patterns of aging. In B. Neugarten (Ed.), *Middle age and aging*. Chicago: University of Chicago Press, 1968.

Heath, D. H. *Maturity and competence: A transactional view*. New York: Halsted, 1977.

Heider, G. M. Vulnerability in infants and young children: A pilot study. *Genetic Psychology Monographs*, 1966, *73*, no. 1, 1–216.

Hoffman, L. W. The employment of women, education, and fertility. *Merrill-Palmer Quarterly*, 1974, *20*, 104–122.

Hoffman, L. W., & Nye, F. I. *Working mothers: An evaluative review of the consequences for wife, husband, and child*. San Francisco: Jossey-Bass, 1974.

Holmes, T. H., & Rahe, R. H. The social readjustment rating scale. *Journal of Psychosomatic Research*, 1967, *11*, 213–218.

Horner, M. Sex differences in achievement motivation and performance in competitive and noncompetitive situations. Unpublished doctoral dissertation, University of Michigan, 1968.

Horner, M. Femininity and successful achievement: A basic inconsistency. In J. M. Bardwick, E. Douvan, M. Horner, & D. Gutman (Eds.), *Feminine personality and conflict*. Monterey, Calif.: Brooks/Cole, 1970.

Horner, M. The motive to avoid success and changing aspirations of college women. In J. Bardwick (Ed.), *Readings on the psychology of women*. New York: Harper & Row, 1972.

Jaensch, E. R. *Der Gegentypus*. Leipzig: Barth, 1938.

Janis, I. Psychological effects of warnings. In G. W. Baker & D. W. Chapman (Eds.), *Man and society in disaster*. New York: Basic Books, 1962.

Janis, I. Vigilance and decision making in personal crises. In G. V. Coelheo, D. A. Hamburg, & J. E. Adams (Eds.), *Coping and adaptation*. New York: Basic Books, 1974.

Janis, I. L., Mahl, G. F., Kagan, J. & Holt, R. R. *Personality: Dynamics, development, and assessment*. New York: Harcourt Brace Jovanovich, 1969.

Janis, I. L., & Mann, L. Coping with decisional conflict. *American Scientist*, 1976, *64* (6), 657–667.

Jones, N. B. Categories of child-child interaction. In N. B. Jones (Ed.), *Ethological studies of child behavior*. London: Cambridge University Press, 1972.

Junod, H. A. *The life of a South African tribe* (2nd ed., 2 vols.). London: Macmillan, 1927.

Kagan, J. American longitudinal research on psychological development. *Child Development*, 1964, *35*, 1–32.

Kagan, J., & Moss, H. A. Stability and validity of achievement fantasy. *Journal of Abnormal and Social Psychology*, 1959, *58*, 357–364.

Kagan, J., & Moss, H. A. *Birth to maturity*. New York: Wiley, 1962.

Keating, D. P. (Ed.). *Intellectual talent: Research and development*. Baltimore: Johns Hopkins University Press, 1976.

Kifer, E. The impact of schooling on perceptions of self. Paper presented at the Self-concept Symposium, Boston, September–October 1978.

Koenig, S. Beliefs and practices relating to birth and childhood among the Galician Ukrainians. *Folk-Lore*, 1939, *50*, 272–287.

Kogan, N. Creativity and cognitive style: A life-span perspective. In P. B. Baltes & K. W. Schaie (Eds.), *Life span developmental psychology: Personality and socialization*. New York: Academic Press, 1973.

Kogan, N., & Pankove, E. Creative ability over a five year span. *Child Development*, 1972, *43*, 427–442.

Kohlberg, L. Stage and sequence: The cognitive-developmental approach to socialization. In D. A. Goslin (Ed.), *Handbook of socialization theory and research*. Chicago: Rand McNally, 1969.

Koriat, A., Melkman, R., Averill, J. R., & Lazarus, R. S. The self-control of emotional reactions to a stressful film. *Journal of Personality*, 1972, *40*, 601–619.

Kotelchuck, M. The nature of the child's tie to his father. Unpublished doctoral dissertation, Harvard University, 1972.

Kotelchuck, M. The infant's relationship to the father: Experimental evidence. In M. E. Lamb (Ed.), *The role of the father in child development*. New York: Wiley, 1976.

Kroeber, T. C. The coping functions of the ego mechanisms. In R. W. White (Ed.), *The study of lives*. New York: Atherton, 1963.

Lamb, M. E. Fathers: Forgotten contributors to child development. *Human Development*, 1975, *18*, 245–266.

Lazarus, R. S. Cognitive and coping processes in emotion. In B. Weiner (Ed.), *Cognitive views of human motivation*. New York: Academic Press, 1974.

Lazarus, R. S. *Patterns of adjustment* (3rd ed.). New York: McGraw-Hill, 1976.

Levinson, D. J. The mid-life transition: A period in adult psychosocial development. *Psychiatry*, 1977, *40* (2), 99–112.

Levinson, D. J., Darrow, C. M., Klein, E. B., Levinson, M. H., & McKee, B. *The seasons of a man's life*. New York: Knopf, 1978.

Levy, M. J., Jr. *The family revolution in modern China*. Cambridge, Mass.: Harvard University Press, 1949.

Lewis, M., & Rosenblum, A. (Eds.). *The effect of the infant on its caregiver*. New York: Wiley, 1974.

Lewis, M., & Weinraub, M. The father's role in the child's social network. In M. E. Lamb (Ed.), *The role of the father in child development*. New York: Wiley, 1976.

Linton, R. Age and sex categories. *American Sociological Review*, 1942, *7*, 589–603.

Lowenthal, M. F., & Haven, C. Interaction and adaptation: Intimacy as a critical variable. *American Sociological Review*, 1968, *33*, 20–30.

Macfarlane, J. W. From infancy to adulthood. *Childhood Education*, 1963, *39*, 336–342.

Macfarlane, J. W. From infancy to adulthood. In M. C. Jones, N. Bagley, J. W. Macfarlane, & M. P. Honzik (Eds.), *The course of human development*. New York: Wiley, 1971, pp. 406–410.

Maddi, S. R. *Personality theories: A comparative analysis*. Homewood, Ill.: Dorsey Press, 1976.

Maddi, S. R. Myth and personality. Paper presented at the annual meeting of the American Psychological Association, Toronto, August 1978.

Maddox, G. L. Persistence of life among the elderly: A longitudinal study of patterns of social activity in relation to life satisfaction. In B. Neugarten (Ed.), *Middle age and aging*. Chicago: University of Chicago Press, 1968.

Mair, L. P. Native marriage in Buganda. Memorandum 19. International African Institute, London, 1940.

Maslow, A. H. *Motivation and personality*. New York: Harper, 1954.

Maslow, A. H. Neurosis as a failure of personal growth. *Humanitas*, 1967, *3*, 153–169. (a)

Maslow, A. H. A theory of metamotivation: The biological rooting of the value-life. *Journal of Humanistic Psychology*, 1967, *7*, 93–127. (b) Reprinted in H. M. Chiang & A. H. Maslow (Eds.), *The healthy personality*. New York: Van Nostrand, 1977.

Maslow, A. H. Toward humanistic biology. *American Psychologist*, 1969, *24*, 724–735.

Masters, W. H., & Johnson, V. E. Human sexual response: The aging male and the aging female. In B. Neugarten (Ed.), *Middle age and aging*. Chicago: University of Chicago Press, 1968.

McClelland, D. C. *Power: The inner experience*. New York: Irvington Press, 1975.

McClelland, D. C., Atkinson, J. W., Clark, R. W., & Lowell, E. L. *The achievement motive*. New York: Appleton-Century-Crofts, 1953.

McClelland, D. C., Davis, W. N., Kalin, R., & Wanner, E. *The drinking man.* New York: Free Press, 1972.

McKeachie, E. J., Doyle, C. L., & Moffet, M. M. *Psychology.* Reading, Mass.: Addison-Wesley, 1976.

Mead, G. H. *Mind, self, and society.* Chicago: University of Chicago Press, 1934.

Mead, M., & Newton, N. Cultural patterning of prenatal behavior. In S. A. Richardson & H. F. Guttmacher (Eds.), *Childbearing—its social and psychological aspects.* Baltimore: Williams & Wilkins, 1967.

Meyer, A. *The commonsense psychiatry of Dr. Adolf Meyer* (A. Lief, Ed.). New York: McGraw-Hill, 1948.

Millham, J., & Jacobson, L. I. The need for approval. In H. London & J. E. Exner (Eds.), *Dimensions of personality.* New York: Wiley, 1978.

Monahan, L., Kuhn, D., & Shaver, P. Intrapsychic versus cultural explanations of the "fear of success" motive. *Journal of Personality and Social Psychology,* 1974, *29* (1), 60–64.

Montemayor, R., & Eisen, M. The development of self perceptions from childhood to adolescence. *Developmental Psychology,* 1977, *13* (4), 314–319.

Morgan, C. D., & Murray, H. A. A method for investigating fantasies. *Archives of Neurological Psychiatry,* 1935, *34,* 289–306.

Moriarty, A. E. *Constancy and IQ change: A clinical view of relationships between tested intelligence and personality.* Springfield, Ill.: Charles C Thomas, 1966.

Moriarty, A. E., & Toussieng, D. W. *Adolescent coping.* New York: Grune & Stratton, 1976.

Murphy, L. B. *Personality in young children.* Vol. 2: *Colin: A normal child.* New York: Basic Books, 1956.

Murphy, L. B., & Moriarty, A. E. *Vulnerability, coping, and growth: From infancy to adolescence.* New Haven, Conn.: Yale University Press, 1976.

Murray, H. A., and collaborators. *Explorations in personality.* New York: Oxford University Press, 1938.

Nauman, T. F. A first report on a longitudinal study of gifted preschool children. *Gifted Child Quarterly,* 1974, *18,* 171–172.

Neugarten, B. L., Moore, J. W., & Lowe, J. C. Age norms, age constraints, and adult socialization. *American Journal of Sociology,* 1965, *70,* 710–717.

Nevin, D. Young prodigies take off under special program. *Smithsonian,* October 1977, pp. 76–82.

Newman, B. M., & Newman, P. R. *Development through life: A psychosocial approach* (2nd ed.). Homewood, Ill.: Dorsey Press, 1979.

Nordby, V. J., & Hall, C. S. *A guide to psychologists and their concepts.* San Francisco: W. H. Freeman, 1974.

Nye, I. *Role structure and analysis of the family.* Beverly Hills, Calif.: Sage, 1976.

Office of Strategic Services Assessment Staff. *Assessment of Men.* New York: Rinehart, 1948.

Ollendick, T. H., & Gruen, G. E. Need for achievement and probability learning. *Developmental Psychology,* 1971, *4,* 165–172.

Osipow, S. H. Vocational behavior and career development, 1975: A review. *Journal of Vocational Behavior,* 1976, *9,* 129–145.

Parsons, T., & Bales, R. F. (Eds.). *Family, socialization, and interaction process.* New York: Free Press, 1955.

Pennebaker, J. W., Burnam, M. A., Schaeffer, M. A., & Harper, D. C. Lack of control as a determinant of perceived physical symptoms. *Journal of Personality and Social Psychology,* 1977, *35* (3), 167–174.

Piaget, J. *The origins of intelligence.* New York: International Universities Press, 1952.

Piaget, J. Intellectual evolution from adolescence to adulthood. *Human Development,* 1972, *15,* 1–12.

Rebecca, M., Hefner, R., & Oleshansky, B. A model of sex role transcendence. *Journal of Social Issues,* 1976, *22,* 197–206.

Rebelsky, F., & Hanks, C. Fathers' verbal interaction with infants in the first three months of life. *Child Development,* 1971, *42,* 63–68.

Riegel, K. F. Adult life crises: A dialectic interpretation of development. In N. Datan & L. H. Ginsberg (Eds.), *Life-span developmental psychology: Normative life crises.* New York: Academic Press, 1975.

Rodman, H. Marital power: The theory of resources in cultural context. *Journal of Comparative Family Studies,* 1972, *3,* 50–69.

Rose, A. M. A current theoretical issue in social gerontology. In B. Neugarten (Ed.), *Middle age and aging.* Chicago: University of Chicago Press, 1968.

Rosen, B. C., & D'Andrade, R. G. The psychological origin of achievement motivation. *Sociometry,* 1959, *22,* 185–218.

Rosenberg, M. *Society and the adolescent self-image.* Princeton, N. J.: Princeton University Press, 1965.

Rosenfeld, G. W. Changing self-esteem by inducing selective attention to successes and failures. Paper presented at the annual meeting of the American Psychological Association, Toronto, August 1978.

Rosenthal, R., & Rosnow, R. L. *Primer of methods for the behavioral sciences.* New York: Wiley, 1975.

Rubin, I. The "sexless older years"—a socially harmful stereotype. *Annals of the American Academy of Political and Social Science,* 1968, *376,* 86–95.

Rule, B. G., & Rehill, D. Direction and self-esteem effects on attitude change. *Journal of Personality and Social Psychology,* 1970, *15,* 359–365.

Sarbin, T. R., & Allen, V. L. Role theory. In G. Lindzey & E. Aronson (Eds.), *Handbook of social psychology* (2nd ed., Vol. 1). Reading, Mass.: Addison-Wesley, 1968.

Schaffer, H. R., & Emerson, D. E. The development of social attachments in infancy. *Monographs of the Society for Research in Child Development,* 1964, *29* (Whole No. 94).

Schapera, I. *The Kliorsan peoples of South Africa.* London: Routledge & Kegan Paul, 1930.

Seagoe, M. V. *Terman and the gifted.* Los Altos, Calif.: Kaufman, 1975.

Sears, P. S., & Barbee, A. H. Career and life satisfaction among Terman's gifted women. In J. Stanley, W. George, & C. Solano (Eds.), *The gifted and the creative: Fifty year perspective.* Baltimore: Johns Hopkins University Press, 1978.

Sears, R. R. Sources of life satisfactions of the Terman gifted men. *American Psychologist,* 1977, *32* (2), 119–128.

Seligman, M. E. P. *Helplessness: On depression, development, and death.* San Francisco: W. H. Freeman, 1975.

Selman, R. L. Taking another's perspective: Role-taking development in early childhood. *Child Development,* 1971, *42,* 1721–1734.

Sheldon, W. H. *The varieties of temperament: A psychology of constitutional differences.* New York: Harper, 1942.

Smith, C. P. The origin and expression of achievement-related motives in children. In C. P. Smith (Ed.), *Achievement-related motives in children.* New York: Russell Sage Foundation, 1969.

Sontag, L. W. Implications of fetal behavior and environment for adult personalities. *Annals of the New York Academy of Sciences,* 1966, *132*(2), 782–786.

Stanley, J. C., Keating, D. P., & Fox, L. H. (Eds.). *Mathematical talent: Discovery, description, and development.* Baltimore: Johns Hopkins University Press, 1974.

Stein, A. H., & Bailey, M. The socialization of achievement orientation in females. *Psychological Bulletin,* 1973, *80,* 346–366.

Stephens, W. N. *The family in cross-cultural perspective.* New York: Holt, Rinehart & Winston, 1963.

Stewart, A. J., & Rubin, Z. Power motivation in the dating couple. *Journal of Personality and Social Psychology,* 1976, *34,* 305–309.

Stewart, A. J., & Winter, D. G. Arousal of the power motive in women. *Journal of Consulting and Clinical Psychology,* 1976, *44,* 495–496.

Sullivan, H. S. *The interpersonal theory of psychiatry.* New York: Norton, 1953.

Tanner, O. *Stress.* New York: Time-Life Books, 1976.

Taylor, I. A. An emerging view of creative actions. In I. A. Taylor & J. W. Getzels (Eds.), *Perspectives in creativity.* Chicago: Aldine, 1975.

Terman, L. M. Introduction. In L. S. Howard, *The road ahead.* Yonkers, N. Y.: World Book, 1941.

Terman, L. M., & Oden, M. H. *Genetic studies of genius.* Vol. 4: *The gifted child grows up: Twenty five years follow-up of a superior group.* Stanford, Calif.: Stanford University Press, 1947.

Terman, L. M., & Oden, M. H. *Genetic studies of genius.* Vol. 5: *The gifted group at mid-life: Thirty five years follow-up of the superior child.* Stanford, Calif.: Stanford University Press, 1959.

Thomas, A., Chess, S., & Birch, H. The origin of personality. *Scientific American,* 1970, *223,* 102–109.

Thompson, S. K. Gender labels and early sex role development. *Child Development,* 1975, *46,* 339–347.

Tittle, C. K., Chitayat, D., & Denker, E. R. Sex role values: A neglected factor in career decision making theory. Paper presented at the 85th annual meeting of the American Psychological Association, San Francisco, August 26–30, 1977.

Torrance, E. P. *Guiding creative talent.* Englewood Cliffs, N. J.: Prentice-Hall, 1962.

Torrance, E. P. *Rewarding creative behavior.* Englewood, Cliffs, N. J.: Prentice-Hall, 1965.

Torrance, E. P. Achieving socialization without sacrificing creativity. *Journal of Creative Behavior,* 1970, *4,* 183–189.

Torrance, E. P. Creativity research in education: Still alive. In I. A. Taylor & J. W. Getzels (Eds.), *Perspectives in creativity.* Chicago: Aldine, 1975.

Torrance, E. P., & Myers, R. E. *Creative learning and teaching.* New York: Dodd, Mead, 1970.

Tresemer, D. W. *Fear of success.* New York: Plenum, 1977.

Trézenem, É. *Notes ethnographiques sur les Tribus Fan du Moyen Ogooné.* Paris: (Gabon) Au Siége de la Société, 1936.

Triandis, H. C. Cross-cultural social and personality psychology. *Personality and Social Psychology Bulletin,* 1977, *3,* 143–158.

Tuddenham, R. D. The constancy of personality ratings over two decades. *Genetic Psychology Monographs,* 1959, *60,* 3–29.

Turnbull, C. M. *The mountain people.* New York: Touchstone/Simon and Schuster, 1972.

Turner, R. H. The real self: From institution to impulse. *American Journal of Sociology*, 1976, *81*, 989–1016.

Turner, R. H., & Gordon, S. Boundaries of the self: The relationship of authenticity to unauthenticity in the self-conception. Paper presented at the Self-concept Symposium, Boston, September–October 1978.

Vaillant, G. E. *Adaptation to life*. Boston: Little, Brown, 1977.

Veroff, J. Development and validation of a projective measure of power motivation. *Journal of Abnormal and Social Psychology*, 1957, *54*, 1–8.

Walberg, H. J. Varieties of adolescent creativity and the high school environment. *Exceptional Children*, 1971, *37*, 111–116.

Wallach, M. A. *The intelligence/creativity distinction*. New York and Morristown, N. J.: General Learning Press, 1971.

Wallach, M. A. Psychology of talent and graduate education. In S. Mersick and associates (Eds.), *Individuality in learning*. San Francisco: Jossey-Bass, 1976.

Weiner, B. Achievement strivings. In H. London & J. Exner, Jr. (Eds.), *Dimensions of personality*. New York: Wiley, 1978.

Weiner, B., & Peter, N. A. Cognitive-developmental analysis of achievement and moral judgments. *Developmental Psychology*, 1973, *9*, 290–309.

Wells, L. E., & Marwell, G. *Self-esteem: Its conceptualization and measurement*. Beverly Hills, Calif.: Sage Publications, 1976.

West, M. M., & Konner, M. J. The role of the father: An anthropological perspective. In M. E. Lamb (Ed.), *The role of the father in child development*. New York: Wiley, 1976.

White, R. W. Strategies of adaptation: An attempt at systematic description. In G. V. Coelheo, D. A. Hamburg, & J. E. Adams (Eds.), *Coping and adaptation*. New York: Basic Books, 1974.

White, R. W. Motivation reconsidered: The concept of competence. *Psychological Review*, 1959, *66*, 297–333.

White, R. W. *The study of lives*. New York: Atherton, 1963.

Whiting, B. B., & Whiting, J. W. M. *Children of six cultures: A psychocultural analysis*. Cambridge, Mass.: Harvard University Press, 1975.

Winter, D. G. *The power motive*. New York: Free Press, 1973.

Winter, D. G., & Stewart, A. J. The power motive. In H. London & J. Exner, Jr. (Eds.), *Dimensions of personality*. New York: Wiley, 1978.

Winter, D. G., Stewart, A. J., & McClelland, D. C. Husband's motives and wife's career level. *Journal of Personality and Social Psychology*, 1977, *35*, 159–166.

Winterbottom, M. R. The relation of need for achievement to learning experiences in independence and mastery. In J. W. Atkinson (Ed.), *Motives in fantasy, action, and society*. New York: Van Nostrand, 1958.

Witkin, H. A., Dyk, R. B., Faterson, H. F., Goodenough, D. R., & Karp, S. A. *Psychological differentiation*. New York: Wiley, 1962.

Wolff, C. T., Friedman, S. B., Hofer, M. A., & Mason, J. W. Relationship between psychological defenses and mean urinary 17-hydroxycorticosteroid excretion rates: I. A predictive study of parents of fatally ill children. *Psychosomatic Medicine*, 1964, *26*, 576–591.

Wolff, P. H. Observations on the early development of smiling. In B. M. Foss (Ed.), *Determinants of infant behavior* (Vol. 2). New York: Wiley, 1963.

Wuebben, P. L., Straits, B. C., & Schulman, G. I. *The experiment as a social occasion*. Berkeley, Calif.: Glendessary Press, 1974.

Zellman, G. L. The role of structural factors in limiting women's institutional participation. *Journal of Social Issues,* 1976, *32,* 33–46.

Zellner, M. Self-esteem, reception, and influenceability. *Journal of Personality and Social Psychology,* 1970, *15,* 87–93.

Ziegarnik, B. On finished and unfinished tasks. In W. D. Ellis (Ed.), *A source book of Gestalt psychology.* New York: Harcourt Brace Jovanovich, 1938.

Name Index

Adams, J. E., 129, 131, 136
Adler, A., 53, 127
Albert, R. S., 30, 127
Allen, V. L., 61, 62, 134
Allport, G. W., 10, 36, 37, 42–46,
     65, 127
Angelino, H. R., 56, 127
Archibald, W., 123, 127
Aronson, E., 134
Astin, A., 15, 127
Atkinson, J. W., 36, 49, 52, 53, 127,
     128, 132, 136
Averill, J. R., 89, 131

Bagley, N., 132
Bailey, M., 51, 135
Baldwin, J., 41
Bales, R. F., 62, 65, 133
Ban, P., 77, 127
Bandura, A., 124, 127
Barbee, A. H., 112, 134
Bardwick, M., 131
Barker, R. G., 15, 74, 127, 128
Bartlett, M., 89, 129
Battit, G., 89, 129
Baumrind, D., 71, 128
Bayley, N., 130
Bernhardt, S., 41
Biddle, B. J., 61, 128
Birch, D., 36, 49, 52, 127, 128
Birch, H., 20, 135
Block, J., 26–28, 128
Bongort, K., 36, 128
Borrow, H., 130
Brim, O. G., Jr., 65, 74, 117, 128

Bronson, W. C., 24, 128
Brown, R., 61, 128
Burnam, M.A., 11, 133
Buro, 13
Buss, A. H., 21, 22, 128

Campbell, A., 124, 128
Cartwright, L. K., 65, 128
Cattell, R. B., 9, 10, 128
Caudill, H. M., 59, 128
Chess, S., 20, 21, 128, 135
Chiang, H. M., 41, 128, 132
Chitayat, D., 73, 135
Chwast, J., 71, 128
Clark, R. W., 52, 132
Clausen, J., 128
Cobb, S., 90, 129
Coelheo, G. V., 129, 131, 136
Cohen, R., 123, 127
Condry, J., 53, 128
Converse, P. E., 124, 128
Cooley, C. H., 117, 128
Cortes, J. O., 65, 128
Coser, R. L., 65, 129
Crowne, D. P., 54, 129
Cumming, E., 54, 55, 129

D'Andrade, R. G., 50, 134
Darley, S., 51, 129
Darrow, C. M., 14, 132
Datan, N., 56, 129, 130, 134
Davis, W. N., 57, 133
de Beauvoir, S., 56, 129
Dellas, M., 30, 129
Denker, E. R., 73, 135

Subject Index